Depression
Constipation
How Pooping Saved My
Sanity...and Other Stories

For all those uniquely brilliant souls, trying to bring laughter back into their lives.

To my friend Naomi, who taught me that I am worth loving all through one question.

And Andrea, my business coach...but most importantly, my friend of constant encouragement and support.

Let's Talk Candidly

A few months ago I had the best poop of my life. In the moment after this poop, I was in complete contentment with life. No word of a lie, I was sure that everything in life was going to be okay. That all struggles I had dealt with would just work out.

Anyone who's had a great poop can surely relate.

It was in this moment - however brief - that I had an epiphany about my depression. To "overcome" depression, something I struggle with everyday, or to at least keep myself moving when all I want to do is stop, is to remember the feeling of complete relief and satisfaction that comes with a really good poop. The "ahhh....at last" moment.

Disgusting? Most likely. But honestly, everyone knows the feeling I'm talking about. And if you don't, eat more veggies and get ready for relaxed relief.

Now, why in the world am I telling you about how pooping made me think about depression? I mean seriously, who thinks about their poop that much?

Well, me. Really, the more I struggled with my depression, the darkness, the fogginess, the need to purge my insides, the more I understood it and tried to find ways to explain it to my support system, those who were empathic, but didn't quite get where my head sat (other than on top of my neck).

When you read my story, you will understand how far into the oily black mire of depression I was really in. What kept me from completely sinking into this darkness was using humour. And in dark places, sometimes humour is at its best. Sometimes off-colour, and sometimes it's just plain funny.

So, be warned! If you don't have a slightly off-colour sense of humour, this may not be the book for you. However, if you want to understand a different side of depression from a completely different point of view, then this could be your cup of tea (or prune juice)!

Number 1 (Not Yet 2): My Pre-Poop Story

All my life, I felt "less than." Less perfect, less smart, less thin, less funny, just less. There's no real reason for this as I grew up in a very good home, with loving parents and a great sister. But, for whatever reason, there was self-hate.

I tried to ignore this self-hate throughout my teen years, but as I started my twenties I "took action" in the hopes of stopping the hate. At the age of 20, I started to starve myself while incessantly swimming as a way to feel prettier and thinner; as a way to feel worthy of love.

Two years later, once I finished university, I had no idea how to keep control of my life in a new world of uncertainty and direction. So, on July 1, yes, Canada's birthday, I purposely threw up my food for the first time. Over the next 7 years, I would purposely throw up on and off whenever I felt as though life was spinning out of control, most often at the end of something in my life - school, relationships, job changes, changing cities, and so on.

While I thought I had this under control, a family death caught me off guard and started my ultimate downward spiral.

My Dad's mom passed away; my sweet-souled Granny. You see, Granny and I shared the same birthday, which made me feel special in my family. With the loss of her heart, her giggle, her preciousness, everything that made me feel special because of our birthday connection, I started to crack. I tried to avoid the grief I was feeling, not just because I lost my Granny, but because I lost a piece of what I believed was my uniqueness. I ignored this by throwing myself into training for a half marathon (and I absolutely HATE running, so this should say something) and getting involved with a couple local musical theatre shows. If you can't think about your feelings because of other commitments, then you don't have to deal with them.

Then, eight months later, my Mom's mother, my Grandmother, passed away at the age of 96. As she was my last remaining grandparent, I was stunned. Up until that point, I had convinced myself that she was actually going to live until 100. Over the next month, I went back to the only coping mechanism that I knew – purging all food. This was the first time that I felt truly alone in my grief. My parents leaned on one another and I really didn't want to cry to them. After all, they had both lost their moms. My sister, while there for support when my Granny passed away, now had her then boyfriend, now husband, to comfort her. So she didn't need to reach out to lean on me like she had previously.

What hit me hardest was when I realized that never again in my life, would I make someone's day simply by calling them. Grandparents are so unique in that their only purpose in your life is to love you. The joy in a grandparent's voice when you talk to them is the most beautiful thing. This realization that the unconditional love they had for me would never be heard again stopped me dead in my tracks. I felt lost.

The grief kept piling up and I kept ignoring it. I went back to my comfortable coping mechanism of throwing up my food and feeling disgusted in who I was as a person.

This continued for a couple of months until one conversation started a chain of events that brought the self-wallowing to a crashing halt.

My dear friend and singer teacher, Naomi, changed a singing lesson into a life lesson when I showed up for my class in less than a singing state of mind. Instead of vocalises and lip trills, we sat on her couch and talked. I talked about what I was doing with my food and about how I was this unlovable thing.

As I poured my heart out, using A LOT of Kleenex in the process, Naomi listened. When I stopped snorting out my words, she said something to me that made me start to question what I was doing. She said, "I'm hearing all this self-hate about yourself. Why do you hate yourself so much?"

I had no answer.

A few weeks later, I still hadn't truly acknowledged that I was depressed and not just grieving. After a fairly normal day at work, I was heading home through downtown Calgary, when I had an all out nervous, very public breakdown in the middle of everything corporate. Somehow, I managed to call a friend, who talked to me as I walked home, and encouraged me to reach out to my boss that evening, letting my boss know what had happened, about my throwing up, and so much more.

I screwed up the courage and sent my boss an email. She immediately called me to offer support in getting help. I thought I was finally on the road to moving through my depression, but that's when the self-hate truly started. I felt like a failure because I couldn't make my way through life with my head held up. I hated admitting defeat in that I couldn't move forward in life and that I actually looked forward to throwing up my food. So…things got worse and I eventually had to take a leave from work.

I guess sometimes you really have to hit rock bottom before you can pick yourself back up.

When I was depressed, I was in a dark hole. I would look at a pin and think, "if I pricked myself, it wouldn't really hurt."

Just in case you're wondering, it does still hurt. A pin's a pin after all...and they are pointy!

Since the actually cutting of myself scared me, I decided that I would stick with control through food. Food was something to be thrown up as soon as I ate it. It most certainly wasn't something to use as nourishment. I would look at food and think, "will this be easy to throw up after?" If so, I ate it. If not, I would find something else.

There were days that I just didn't want to exist. It's not that I wanted to die, although a little part of me considered it quite often, it's more that I just wanted to stop being. And I was sure that no one would notice, even though I had people around me who wanted to help.

I guess that must have gotten through to some part of my brain, because I started reaching out for help and found a great counsellor, who happened to comment that I had a unique way of looking at the world; that there were some humorous insights into my background and story. "Perhaps," she suggested, "you should try writing these stories down."

So...I did. And that's when it happened. I started seeing life from that brand new angle.

I thought about the stories in my life, from childhood right through to my breakdown in a very public place, and more often than not I laughed at something in the experience. The obvious, the ridiculous, the absurd, the shocking, and the merely mundane. Then I began to write and slowly, I started taking real control of my life back, not food control.

The more humour I looked for, the more my mental clarity improved. I felt myself becoming lighter.

Over the next year, my interactions with people became more about creating stories through dialogue and communication. When I took the time to talk to people and listen to their uniqueness I noticed more about them and the great things in my day.

The dark hole I felt stuck in started to become more of a shallow pit. My thoughts became less hateful. Don't get me wrong, I still had - and have - negative thoughts, but the self-loathing, the unworthiness that resonated so loudly in my skull, became quieter with each story.

Laughter, however small, helped begin the healing of my soul. And this is why, when I had the amazing poop I did that one day, that I decided that it was time to help bring some soul healing to others. I hope that by showing where I was able to find laughter will help guide you to your own...or at the very least help you understand how to poop a bit better.

The last day that I purposely threw up was August 22, 2011. As soon as I finished, I remember consciously thinking out loud, "Enough is enough. No more." And every day since has been a challenge. Every day. But it's a challenge I accept and I look for the things that will make me laugh, and am transforming the shallow pit into a divot (I am only human).

Smile on my face, toilet paper in hand, I'm ready to tackle the world.

The Poop Connection

Back to the Great Poop: My Internal Movement.

When I had this amazing, "ah-ha" inspiring poop moment, I thought, why not share what depression can be like with others? At least to some degree.

In essence, being depressed is like being in a state of constant constipation. The only way to move through it is in baby steps, with a wee bit of grunting, and recognizing that "movement" doesn't happen overnight.

For you to see exactly where I'm coming from, let's take a loosky, shall we? Below, I have created a handy dandy little chart for you that shows how depression and constipation are a lot alike.

Depression	Constipation
• Thoughts are dark	• Poop is dark (hopefully)
• Meaningful thoughts don't flow	• Poop really doesn't flow
• Brain feels full (cotton brain)	• Bum feels full (sticky bum)
• You feel numb	• Parts can go numb
• Heavy feeling	• Feeling heavy
• Distended Reality	• Distended Belly
• Terrifying thoughts	• Terrifying cramps
• Sometimes drugs are needed	• Sometimes oil is needed
• Feel emotionless	• Feel lethargic
• Spend lots of time in bed, internal struggle	• Spend lots of time on toilet, internal struggle
• Can induce tears	• Can induce tears
• Feeling of hopelessness	• Feeling of endlessness

- Plead for a change
- You feel stuck / stopped
- Daily struggle
- Ringing in ears (tinnitus)

- Verbal stutter

- And so on...

- Plead for movement
- You are stuck / stopped
- Body struggle
- Bum ringing (gas escape)

- Bum stutter – rabbit poops

- And so on...

Hopefully you get the picture... just not too visual though!

Being able to explain what "depression" felt like in a way that could make things a bit more clear helped immensely in my relationships and in building a better support system. Many people thought I was "just sad" and should buck up. Being sad was farthest from the truth. When I went through the above comparisons, people were better able to understand what was going through my mind and that it actually had nothing to do with being "sad." It was more about something not working right in my body.

Try it – next time someone is trying to understand just how depression is affecting you, tell them it's not about being sad. It's about being brain constipated.

Number 2: The Stories

The following are a few of the stories that helped me regain movement in my brain. Better flow because I was remembering how to laugh. From these stories, I learned life lessons that still help me recognize why I'm not alone in life and why we're really just a funny story from moving forward.

While the stories are meant to entertain you, I've also pulled out a few of the bigger lessons from each story. Hopefully, you'll be able to use these lessons in your own life on your road to fluid movement.

Side note: all names, with the exception of Robin and Andy, have been changed.

Smart Poop & Other Bathroom Stories

Everybody poops - why not take a moment and focus on what we have in common...even if it's a bodily function.

Saskatchewan Poop Taxi

Incredibly science-oriented, my older sister, Robin, naturally gravitated towards a career where she could use her left-brain on a regular basis by becoming a Public Health Inspector.

While I tend to get a little grossed out by some of the stories she tells me about restaurants, pools, and other public spaces, there is one story that sticks out.

One year, there was a Norwalk virus outbreak in a retirement home. As such, samples of poop of the affected residents were collected. My sister's role in the entire breakout? Delivering the stool samples to the proper individuals who would assess them.

Essentially, my sister became a Poop Taxi for a day.

As she was telling me this, I kept thinking, "there's got to be a way that Robin could take more initiative in helping with her role."

When her birthday came around that year, I decided to give her Josh Richman and Anish Sheth's book, *What's Your Poo Telling You*. In her card, I said that the next time she was required to taxi poop around, she would be able to have an assessment for the lab techs.

She had a huge giggle at the book…but never actually used it as a way to show more initiative in her role.

The next year? I gave her the follow up book, *What's My Pee Telling Me?*, which, in my opinion, should have been book number one in the series.

For some reason when she opened the gift, she wasn't as impressed as she was the year before...

I Swear I Shower

During the summer that my depression took hold of my entire being, I made two commitments to myself: every day I was to 1) to shower and 2) leave my apartment for at least 5 minutes. To ensure that I was getting out of the house and not sitting at home, I would go to coffee shops to read and write while enjoying coffee and people watching. However, what happened at these coffee shops made me paranoid that I might only be showering in my mind each morning.

It all started innocently enough with the coffee shop leaving its outside door open to let the cool breeze through; little did they know that it would let in a fly. Somehow, sitting in the back corner of the shop, the fly was able to make its way to me and disrupt my reading for the next 30 minutes. I thought it was going to be a one-time thing, completely unaware that this would continue for the rest of the summer, every time I went into any coffee shop and restaurant from there on out.

While on dates in high-end restaurants, the flies would come. While drinking coffee from a sippy cup, the flies would come. While eating a muffin through the cellophane, they would still come. As I wandered the streets, followed by my ever-present swarm of flies, I kept thinking, why me? Why did they keep coming to me?! I shower...right? I'm cleanly, aren't I?

I could feel my inner Hulk beginning to build and was worried that one day I would simply snap and start swatting at flies that weren't even there. My hair going wild, nostrils flaring, eyes crossed and my arms flailing about in the hopes of hitting and killing all the little flies in this world. My friends started joking that they were going to buy me a fly swatter to carry around with me. While I laughed along on the outside, I was inwardly secretly hoping that they would buy me one. My own special weapon, much like Thor's hammer, that I could use to rid this world, or at least the air around me, of incessant buzzing.

It wasn't until I joined a Meetup group for freelancers where I snapped. This group met at a coffee shop (naturally) and would work together for a few hours to avoid the isolation that can happen when you work at home. The first time I went to this group, things were going super swell when out of nowhere a fly landed on my writing pad. I unblinkingly stared at it for about a minute, hoping that no one else would see the fly's attraction to me and the red flashing behind my eyes. When I looked up, one of the guys in the group said to me "flies - they're always here." I sighed and said to him "Really? I thought it was me and I was worried you folks would think I didn't shower."

He so kindly told me that the flies were there all the time and that it really wasn't me and he believed that I did shower. Although he never sat across from me again. In fact, he actually moved right across the country a couple months after our meeting. Still trying not to take this too personally.

Since then I've been able to relax a bit, knowing that my morning showers are actually happening. Rather, I've shifted my thinking and acknowledge that come hell or high water...or nuclear war, the flies will still always be there.

Smelly Eyes

It is no secret that I believe that flies are out to get me. I have spent many a night wide awake, staring up at my mosquito netting, thinking that my ultimate downfall will be because of flies.

Unfortunately, in my early days of moving through my "it's not me" fly phase, I had an incident that squashed my progress. I hadn't had a fly land on my coffee or buzz around my head in a few weeks, when I decided to go back to my favourite coffee shop. It was there, back at my place of refuge, where I was coming out of the washroom when a fly flew right into my open eye. This completely startled me, so much so that I bumped into, and then bounced off of the wall. Much like a pin-ball machine, my body was unceremoniously flung from item to item as I blinked the shock away. Thankfully not too many people saw this happen, which is a blessing. I mean, I already had very little dignity at this coffee shop as I had fallen up their booth stairs, spilt coffee on my table and their sugar stand, and accidentally taken someone else's order on more than one occasion.

When I got back to my table, I sent a text to my friend Julie letting her know that the flies were back and that they were now attacking my eyes. The conversation went as follows:

Me: Oh my gosh...I just had a fly hit my eyeball. So creepy!

Julie: Do your eyes stink?! ;P

Me: Maybe...but I can't twist my nose that way to see if they smell!

Julie: Okay. Here's the plan. Ask whoever is nearest you to please sniff your cornea.

Me: Hahahaha! Could you imagine if I did that?! That's pretty much a Just for Laughs gag right there!

Julie: :D We should go into business

For the next half hour, I kept envisioning myself going up to people asking them if they could smell my eyes since I just had a fly hit one of them. All I could see in my head were these confused, judging, and nervous faces as people slowly turned and walked away from me.   Really, what other response would someone have to this type of question from a stranger?

Then I started imagining people leaning in closely and taking a gigantic whiff of my eye. This made me laugh out loud, resulting in many a head turning to look at me in my corner booth. I couldn't even play it off as though I was reading a funny book since I was reading Stieg Larsson's, *Girl With the Dragon Tattoo*. Not exactly light reading. Clearly, it was a low dignity day at the coffee shop.

Moving forward, short of spraying myself with fly spray every time I leave the house, I've come to a few solutions to ensure that the flies never come near me again, namely:

- Increase showering to 3 times a day
- Find some über strong deodorant and apply multiple times daily, and
- Figure out how to get my eyes all soapy clean. I'm thinking Dove soap bar. After all, it worked when I had my mouth washed out when I was younger when I said dirty words, why wouldn't it work for cleaning up my eyes? An added bonus? The 1/4 moisturizer in the bar would make my eyelashes super soft!

Keeping my fingers crossed that this new routine will work ASAP.

Deep Stretching

My whole life I've been a fairly reserved individual when it comes to being in groups of people. In fact, most people think I'm mute until we're one on one. I don't really say much unless I feel that something needs to be said.

One day back in Grade 12, I was going out to Second Cup with a couple of close friends, when I found out that four other girls would be joining us. I knew that I would be fairly quiet on the conversation side of things, and would just enjoy listening to tales the gals would tell.

As we enjoyed our white mochas - with whipped cream, of course - my friend Chelsea began telling a story about one of her ex-boyfriends, which went a little, like this:

One day she was at his house, waiting in his bedroom while he finished taking a shower. All of a sudden the phone rang and he came bounding out of the bathroom, ran across his bedroom, completely buck naked, except for a lone towel. Unfortunately, the towel was not very secure and fell off mid-stride, giving Chelsea an eyeful that she hadn't yet experienced.

Chelsea then began to describe his body to the group, something that many a 16 and 17-year-old gal would be curious about. She described everything as seeming to be a bit stretched sideways; almost as though there was an extra vertical insert throughout his entire body, with the exception of one thing, the part that the lone towel was once covering. As we all giggled thinking about this boy's lack of endowment, I lost my inhibitions about speaking up in a group and blurted out, "Well...I guess not everything stretched."

The rest of the group looked at me went silent, realizing what I, the quiet one had said, then re-burst into hysterics. One of the new additions to this group, Callie, grabbed my hand and said, "I guess still waters really do run deep!"

Of course, none of us were able to look the boy in the...eye when we were back at school.

Relationship Markers

When I first started dating my fella, Andy, we spent a lot of time together right away, just laughing, cooking and enjoying one another's company.

A few weeks into our relationship we had hit many a relationship marker because of the amount of time we were spending together. Things like jacket shopping, support through a funeral, knee surgery, wedding attendance and much more, but we had yet to experience the one marker that can make or break a budding romance. The one that everyone knows is coming, but secretly dreads...the "Fart Marker."

That's right, neither of us had released air yet.

To this day, Andy tells me that I do this cute little dance where I look like a penguin. My hands look like penguin flippers and I flap them at my sides. It's often a source of enjoyment for him...and me I suppose. In fact, this "dance" is apparently what first caught his attention. Although, I still argue that I don't waddle when I dance. I'm more of a loose goose.

One morning, while modeling his new winter jacket for me, Andy decided to flap his arms in the fashion that I dance. The penguin flap, if you will. As his arms were coming down on the third flap, he flapped out a fart at the same time.

Up to this point, Andy had never been one to become embarrassed. In fact, he loves being the centre of attention, and the more eyes that are on him, the better. However, when he realized that he just Penguin Farted, his faced went bright red - a shade of red I didn't know existed. I automatically burst out laughing, trying to hold back some tears since I had just finished my makeup. He ran behind me and buried his head on my shoulder blades...not wanting me to see the embarrassment that my manly man could have.

This has since become known as the Penguin Fart. At first I hoped that he would remember the embarrassment he felt as he released his manly air into the world and try to keep his bodily noises to himself...but I was wrong.

Many years, Penguin Farts, and what are now known as my Whale Burps, later, our relationship markers have been blown out of the water.

Romanian Dancing & Foreign Smells

Having known my friend Jaime since we were 7, we decided that once we graduated university we would take off for foreign adventures in the faraway lands of Europe. Having developed the closest of friendships, we shared all our secrets, crushes, clothes...and body functions.

You see Jaime was a supreme farter.

We don't know why, she was just the gassiest gal. Lovely, but gassy. One night before our Europe adventure, Jaime warned me that on foreign food, her gas might become uncontrollable. Of course, as she was telling me this, she had just let some air go and was laughing so hard that tears were coming down her face. I knew what was coming in the months ahead.

Throughout our whole trip she had been doing really well. I was so proud of her, not disturbing the foreign lands with the smells of a Canadian. Yet, this all changed once we hit Cluj in Romania. On our first night there, a group of 10 from our tour decided to go out, explore the town, and find a place to dance. Luckily, we found the perfect club and started dancing up a storm on a jam-packed dance floor. As only two awkward, goofy Canadian gals can, we were having a ball doing our "sexy" moves (shopping cart, mow the lawn, water sprinkler...you all know them...admit it), when Jaime decided that she was going to throw her hands in the air and spin around.

As she was spinning, she let go a foreign fart that no one could hear. She continued spinning, with a sly smile on her face, to spread the smell around a little. Only someone who had known her for 15 years would understand what the smile meant and be able to prepare for what was coming. As the smell broadened its range, the entire dance floor cleared off. All except for Jaime. She stood there in the middle of the dance floor, laughing so hard...and with a look of pride on her face.

As people were gasping for air and waiting for the smell to dissipate, Jaime proudly marched over to the corner where our group was and announced, "Hee hee. It was me!"

This was a moment I knew that I was truly proud of my friend. She was always one to take responsibility for her actions, without being embarrassed of what the action may have been.

Jaime taught me a lot on this trip, but none as important as fully embracing who you are, mind, body, and smell!

Potty-training or Why I Only Babysat Once in My Life

When you turn 11 in St. Albert, Alberta, you are allowed to sign up for a Babysitter's Course where you learn all sorts of topics that will help you become an excellent babysitter. At the end of this course, your name is then added into the City of St. Albert's babysitter referral program. From there, you can babysit, with parents feeling awesome that you are fully equipped to look after their namesakes.

I was stoked when I was finally able to take this course. Not so much because I liked kids (I didn't), but because my older sister took the course and I wanted to do every thing that she did. After all, while she's been shorter than me since I was eight, she has always been the idol that I look up to.

After successfully completing the course, I was given my Babysitter Certificate card, and was ready for my first babysitting experience.

My moment of babysitting independence came 4 months later. My sister's best friend, Cathy, accidentally double booked her babysitting self and asked if I could take one of her jobs. It was for a two-and-a-half-year-old girl, named Sarah, so it didn't seem like too hard a job. Perfect for my first time, right?

What Cathy conveniently forgot to mention as she told me about the job was that:

- Sarah was just being potty trained, and
- She had diarrhea.

Potty training I could deal with. This had been covered in training. Diarrhea had not.

About a half hour after Sarah's parents left was when everything started, umm, moving. Every 15 - 20 minutes for the next 3 hours, I was running Sarah to the washroom, coaching her through these sessions of life.

Exhausted, and a little bit dehydrated, things seemed to calm down and Sarah was able to fall asleep. After a final clean up, I collapsed on the couch and waited for my employers to come home.

Exhausted, I silently cursed the Babysitter's Course, as there was never a section on how to deal with a potty training, diarrhea inflicted child! Yes, they taught you how to change diapers, feed a baby, make snacks and many first aid scenarios, but they never warn you about explosive poop, constant diaper changings, and how to handle...smells.

I was simply overwhelmed and just wanted to leave. I cursed Cathy for double booking her calendar. I cursed Sarah's parents for saying that she was getting over "a small upset stomach" (hello understatement). I cursed myself for going against my initial feelings of not really liking kids and wanting to be like my sister.

While the babysitting job lasted only four hours in total, they were the longest four hours of my life. By the time Sarah's parents arrived home I had made a promise to myself:

Never again will I, Lindsay Harle, babysit. I will steer clear of diapers and any beings that may need them. There is simply no amount of money worth a potty training, diarrhea having 2-year old. Never again.

And, over 20 years later, I have never babysat again. Really, this type of trauma is one that stays with you and wakes you up in the middle of the night. For the rest of my life, I will be haunted, hearing the cries of two-year-old Sarah saying, "I don't feel so well."

Boyfriend Giggles, a Unicorn and a Penguin

On my road to depression fluidity, I realized that my stories had one thing in common...that I actually have the maturity of a 12 year old. Why? Well, namely because I find awkward farting situations hilarious.

When I first started dating Andy, I realized that our maturity level might be on the same level after I received the below few texts from him.

The year that Andy and I started dating, my friend had given me a unicorn Pillow Pet – now named Lucky – for Christmas. While I initially tried to hide Lucky when Andy came over. I soon stopped realizing that if he didn't like it, then he would just have to deal. Just as I expected, when Andy saw Lucky lying on my bed, he made fun of me for having this "child's" toy...but stopped once he realized how awesome a pillow it actually was. I mean, they're so comfy!

Shortly after Andy discovered Lucky, he had to go in for knee surgery. To keep him company in the hospital and bring a smile to his face, I found him a penguin pillow pet (remember – Penguin Farts). As soon as he saw the penguin, he named it Mr. Penguin because Mr. Penguin was so fancy in his tuxedo.

When Andy left the hospital, he was pretty certain his dog would eat the penguin if we brought it to his place, so we simply left Mr. Penguin at my place. Every time Andy came over, he would promptly find Mr. Penguin and snuggle right up.

Having had the Farting Relationship Marker a few months back, Andy decided that he would no longer hold his farts in and would just keep on going whenever he was at my place. So much so, that Andy started to blame any farts on Lucky.

One day, I received the following text sequence from Andy:

I just farted mmmmm

Ya u did....Gross

I burst out laughing, giggling until my eyes started to tear up. The looks on both the unicorn and the penguin made these simple texts pure comedy gold.

While I'm not saying this is the moment that I knew Andy would be in my life for a while, it certainly was a moment that I knew I found my partner for bad humour.

Love Defined.

A few months after Andy and I moved in together, he became violently sick. Having to go to emergency two nights in a row after seeing blood in his vomit (mmm mmm mmm), I was scared beyond belief and stressed that I had no idea what was going on with my fella.

Thankfully, he was soon on the mend without any major complications.

Once back home, he quickly became the carefree guy that I had started dating. So much so, that the first night back from the hospital, I crawled into bed around 11:00 pm and simply looked at him while he slept. As I look at my sleeping fella, I kept thinking "isn't he so cute. I am so lucky to have him and that he's going to be ok. My heart is full."

Just as I finished my thought, Andy rolled over and picked his nose in his sleep.

Love and grossness: nothing sums up our relationship more than this moment ever will.

Poop Lessons: It Doesn't Always Stink

- There's always room to be assertive / proactive in your career...even with a little poop.
- No one is aware as you are about your body and its...smells.
- Sometimes not everything in life stretches...and that's okay. It's more about what can be done without the stretching.
- Relationships really only begin when you let all your air out...even if by accident.

Puns and Randomness!

Puns are the most amazing thing in the world. You can make practically anything in a conversation a pun, and bring a bit more humour to your life.

For instance, I have a client who deals with retaining wall blocks. One day, while we scheduled a meeting, he stated that his next day was pretty full. I of course replied with, "Don't you mean, you're pretty blocked in?" I could hear his eye roll over the phone, but knew he appreciated the amazing pun I just spouted.

See – giggles in any situation.

Thirteen Inches and a Polish Date!

A few years back I was dating a Polish fellow named Milo; nothing serious, just some fun times and lots of laughs.

On one of our dates, we decided to play it low key and have a movie night in. Since he still lived at home and I was in my own apartment, it made the most sense for him to come over to my place.

Having never been to my place before, Milo decided to have a look around and see what treasures my apartment contained.

When he walked into my living area, he was in for the surprise of his life. Not being a collector of the newest TV technology out there, I still had my itty-bitty 13-inch television set. Since it suited my entertainment needs, I never once thought of buying a bigger one.

As Milo sat down on the couch, he kept making fun of how tiny my television was, when he finally asked, "Just how big is it?" To which I replied, "13 inches."

Milo's response was, "13 inches? Wow, that's small!" I looked him dead in the eye and said, "Milo, sometimes all a girl needs is 13 inches."

Not expecting such a blunt quip, he blushed and didn't say anything more about my pint-sized television. For the rest of the night, he was tight lipped and seemed rather bashful.

We didn't date much more after that. In all honesty, I think my 13 inches intimidated Milo. Poor thing.

A couple weeks later I was having dinner with my folks and family friends where I retold this story. When finished, my

Dad held up his wine glass and exclaimed with a huge smile on his face, "That's my girl!"

My Dad's been proud of me plenty of times in my life, but I have never seen pride on his face like that night. I guess it's plain to see where my random humour came from...genetics!

Bubble Wrap Joy!

When I pop bubble wrap, I feel nothing except pure, uncensored joy. Popping bubbles is my ultimate happy place. Bubble wrap brings back memories of childhood innocence when a simple popping of a bubble would bring hours of entertainment.

To this day, this is honestly one of my favourite past times.

Recently, I was chatting with a friend about my love for bubble wrap. To support this love, my friend sent me an email with the most exciting thing I have ever seen: a bubble wrap calendar!

After taking a moment to catch my breath from being overwhelmed by this newfound item, I remembered a conversation I had with an old co-worker a few years back. I was chatting with my colleague Doug about how I had just purchased some new, awesome IKEA patio furniture. I was all geared up to create my own patio oasis, but the weather we were having just wasn't agreeing with my plans. Rain every day, grey clouds galore, and a ridiculous wind that gusted even the tightest of A-line skirts up.

It was then that Doug and I had a conversation between our cubicle wall:

Me: I just bought the best patio furniture. I can't wait to use it and sit on my balcony, reading all day long!

Doug: Oh yeah - that's exciting. Pints, patios and reading. Awesome times!

Me: Yeah...but the weather isn't really cooperating with me. It is sooooo cold out that I can't sit outside without freezing!

Doug: Well, you could buy a heating lamp and put that on your balcony too. All you would need is a really long extension cord to plug it in and there - heat!

Me: Hmm....OR I could get a blanket made of bubble wrap and fill it with hot Jell-O! It's brilliant!!

Crickets

Me: Doug?

Doug: Where in the world did you get that idea? You are so random!

Me: What? It's brilliant AND fun!

Doug: Uh-huh...well...good luck!

Me: Don't need luck with this superb idea!

Truly, only a person who has the purest of innocence (or brain function) could come up with the random idea of a Jell-O-filled bubble wrap blanket.

Fortunately, the bubble wrap calendar tells me that there are people who love bubble wrap as much as I do. This calendar is the first step to making my bubble wrap warm blankie vision come true.

Update: I'm still working on this invention since hot Jell-O is actually just hot water with gelatin in it. All is still a work in progress.

The Coffee-Cough Adventure

I have a habit of always succumbing to a head cold during cold and flu season. While these head colds are always a bit of a frustration, I do have to say that I (not so secretly) enjoy the sexy voice I have during these times.

One time, when I was on recovery from one of these colds, everything was finally clearing up, with the exception of a rather annoying lingering cough. I had spent nights coughing, with little success of true cough satisfaction, although my abs of steel had started to develop.

After one long night of coughing, I decided that enough was enough. I had to get out of my apartment and decided to venture out to my favourite little coffee shop, get some work done, and have some human interaction. The minute I sat down though I started to cough up a storm; very embarrassing for myself and a plain nuisance for those around me. I felt so bad for the poor people around me at the coffee shop as they were slowly inching their chairs farther and farther away from me.

To keep myself company as I became more and more isolated, I texted my friend and said to her that I think I may have just hacked up a lung in the coffee shop. Just as my heart was sinking lower in embarrassment, my friend responded with:

Don't you mean the "Coughy Shop?!"

Shooting coffee out my nose the minute I read this, my cough was immediately gone! Turns out all I needed to cure my cough were a pun and some snorts to clear everything up. True, I may have done some damage to my poor throat and nose, but sometimes you have to take a bit of the pain to get healthy.

Dead Sea Sprint

Forget Halloween! Christmas is the scariest time of year...at least for those of use who aren't particularly fond of the mall in the first place. This is the time of year when numerous commissioned sales people stand in the middle of the mall, asking you to try a sample of their hand cream, super drinks, chocolate, free gifts and so much more.

I understand why they're fairly aggressive (hello commissions), but I always feel highly pressured when talking to them. I'm reminded of the markets in Cuba where, before you know it, the sales guy has your name engraved on wooden trinkets, meaning you have to buy them. (I may have had a lesson or two to learn about sharing my name with strangers after they call me "pretty lady.")

I've learned that, when walking past them, DO NOT make eye contact, but if I do, smile, say no thanks, look straight ahead and quickly walk away before being pulled in with their entrancing eyes and plastered smiles.

One year, I found a kindred Scary Mall spirit in my friend, Cindy. During one of our cawfee tawks, we discovered that we both had unsettling feelings about malls, particularly malls during the holidays specifically because of the commissioned sales mannequins.

To avoid the mall's "most wonderful time of year," Cindy and I decided to escape the city and head to beautiful Banff, where we thought commissioned sales people wouldn't be able to find us. We just wanted to enjoy the crisp, clean air, the view of the mountains, Welch's Chocolate Shop (mmm...candy corn) and just a relaxing day out of Calgary.

As we were getting ready to leave our wonderful day behind, we went into the basement of the mall where Shoppers Drug

Mart was located to buy a pop for the mini road trip back to Calgary. Heading to the Shoppers, we heard a voice calling out to us from our right side saying, "Hello, would you like to try a sample..."

I began to look in the hopes that they would be sampling chocolates, when Cindy forcefully grabbed my left arm and started pulling me into an all out sprint. She gasped out to me "No - keep going. Those are the Dead Sea salt scrub people who will never let you go until you buy something! Just keep going and don't look back." It felt very adventure movie, running for our lives. Knees up, arms pumping, aliens chasing us to our certain doom.

Curious, I looked back to see the sales guy standing, watching us with a confused look as to what just happened. Clearly, I would be the one killed off in a horror movie because of this curiosity.

As the sales gent and I made eye contact, I had the feeling that he had never had potential customers take off in a Usain Bolt-type sprint to avoid being swept into his hypnotic trance and voice, while teaching the benefits of the Dead Sea salts. While seeing the shocked look on this fellow's face almost made me feel sorry for him, it wasn't enough for me to go back and try (AKA: end up buying) the scrub.

Needless to say...I was definitely disappointed that they weren't chocolate samples, but very glad that Cindy kept me safe from having to try out a product I really didn't want, but wouldn't be able to say "no" to.

On a side note, I've never been happier that I'm a sprinter when I need to be.

"A" High Pelvic Thrust

People are often shocked to find out that I love to sing. That, growing up, I took lessons, completed my Royal Conservatory exams, and went to an "artsy-fartsy" high school where Musical Theatre was my favourite class.

For me, particularly when trying to climb out of a dark place, singing is one of the most cathartic things I have ever been able to do.

Now, that said, I have never been a true soprano. Trust me, those Mariah Carey notes are not something that should be coming from me. Rather, I would say that I am a high alto; altos get the more interesting parts in choirs anyways..

However, to keep stretching myself, my singing teacher, Naomi, suggested I learn *Pie Jesu* from Andrew Lloyd Webber's *Requiem*. When we decided on this, I was hoping that she would take the top of the duet, and I, the bottom so that we wouldn't scare her poor cat during our lesson. No such luck! Forever encouraging me to expand my comfort zone, Naomi was adamant that I sing the soprano part to stretch my range and, as she told me, I *could* do it. I was just a bit too scared to try. After all, sometimes hearing your own voice can be a frightening thing.

One day when we were rehearsing the song, I was having problems hitting the high A on pitch and was beginning to get frustrated with myself. Finally, I had a great idea that would take my mind off of hitting the note and help to propel myself to being on pitch.

As I was singing, I prepped myself, firmly grounding my feet, placing them shoulder width apart, arms loose at my sides, throat open, and chest proudly out. Just as I sang the high A, I did one of the biggest pelvic thrusts I've ever done. Sure enough, I hit the note beautifully, with tons of energy to keep going through the line and didn't even think of how high it was for me.

I was so proud.

The only problem? As I was mid-pelvic thrust, Naomi burst into hysterics. With laughing tears streaming down her face, she gasped, "What was that? You can't ever do that in a performance!"

To which I responded, with a very cheeky smile on my face, "I know. It was just to take my mind off of hitting the high note...and I finally got it, didn't I? Now I know that I *CAN* do it."

Touché!

To my knowledge, Natalie hasn't used this Pelvic Technique™ with any of her other students. Something about it being a little too "R" rated for her studio.

Orca...Whales?

Not the most brilliant of eight-year-olds, I was very gullible as a child (ok...I still am, but have definitely upped the wattage in my brain's light bulb). This would often have me asking odd and very random questions of my parents and sister just so I could know what was and wasn't true.

On one of our ski trips at this tender age, my family and I were driving back from the ski hill to the hotel, when out of the blue, I asked, "Are Killer Whales dolphins or whales because I heard that they were dolphins."

After a quick moment of silence and "the look" between my parents in the front of the car – you know the one; the one of "Oh God, will she be able to live a normal life when she's older without us?" – my science fanatic sister piped up and said in her "I know! I'm brilliant" voice, "They're whales. Their scientific name is Orca."

My Dad, ever the quick-witted responder, promptly said, "So the ones that spit must be Horcas! Hahaha!"

Deafening silence was heard from my mom, as she rolled her eyes. A disgusted throat cluck came from my sister. And I, well I laughed right along with my dad, right until tears came down my cheeks.

Reflecting back on my life, I've pinpointed this as the moment I realized my humour would forever be childish and puns would become my life guides.

NOTE: It's okay to groan at this joke. I know...I still do, but I absolutely love it. Groaning laughter is still laughter after all.

Musical Theatre and iPhone 4s

I'm going to be honest. When it comes to technology, I'm a bit of a slut (in the best way possible). I have never been a "brand" lover, going for whichever laptop or smartphone best suited my needs (and price range). Then...I was introduced to the iPhone 4 and my life changed.

I fell in love with the camera, the battery power, the ability to Face Time with my family (once my Dad figured out how to use his iPhone), the apps, and so much more. Everything about it was perfect. Everything except for one small thing...the autocorrect when texting.

My phone, let's call him Hubert, would come up with the most random autocorrects. Changing works to ducks, hugs, clocks, supercalifragilisticexpialidocious (seriously – I'm not kidding), and so on.

However, I never expected Hubert to change words to composers. One day, I was walking down the street, splitting my attention between my feet and the sidewalk with my face and iPhone screen, texting my friend to plan our evening. I was trying to type the word "sending," but accidentally hit an "o" instead of an "e." My iPhone, realizing that "sonding" wasn't a real word, decided that, what I was clearly trying to type was the word "Sondheim" because, really, what iPhone user wouldn't be trying to type "Sondheim?"

To me, Hubert should have changed it to "sounding" or even "sending," but I knew there was something different about Hubert the moment I he entered my life. After all, he wasn't anything like the many phones I had before.

When I realized that Sondheim was the autocorrect word of choice, I got a big smile on my face and felt my heart warm a little since, as a lover of Sondheim musicals, I was proud that

Hubert was so well versed in musical theatre terminology. So much so, that Sondheim – a word that I had never typed into Hubert's brain before – was his go-to word.

Of course, I know Hubert wasn't the true brain behind his autocorrecting abilities. Naturally, my interest has been piqued, wanting to know more about the programmers of the iPhone. With "Sondheim" being in their database, I think we've all learnt a bit about the personalities and extracurriculars of the employees outside of the Apple halls.

Cars and Emus

Whenever I drive I notice license plates and try to make words out of the three letters. Not sure why, but probably because I like to make sense of things. I love it when I drive past a car and the three letters already form a word, like "HUG" or "LUV."

In fact, at my old apartment, the two cars who parked closest to me, had the letters on their plates as follows: TUF and LUV. For four years, I parked my car beside TUF LUV...and I became all the stronger for it.

Now, when I see unintentional words on plates, I do an inner happy dance. Of course, this has to be an inner dance...I am driving after all. If I were to wiggle my hips, stretch my arms, and swirl my hair around, swerving across lanes would most likely happen and the nightly news would have a headline of "Car Dancer Crashes Because Hips Did Lie." But, in my inner dance, my heart is gleeful, recognizing that these license plates are there just for me...and not by law.

When I was last in the market for a new car, I had to have an internal chat about keeping my eyes on the road and not on licence plates. To ensure that I would remain focused, I brought Andy with me on all test drives. We had only been dating a couple of months at the time and I hadn't yet shown him my entire repertoire of car "moves." Plus, he understood all the "car speak," so could ask the technical questions that didn't surround, "how well does this seat support gyrating hips?"

On our very first test drive, Andy, Owen (the car dealer), and I were driving along, (me driving, Andy in the passenger and Owen in the backseat) enjoying the quick 15-minute jaunt, when a car came speeding past us.

As this speedster passed, the license plate's letters read **EMU**. I got so excited as I had never seen a license plate spell **EMU** before. I giddily said to Andy and Owen, "Look! That license plate spells Emu. Get it? **Emu**? Like the fast running bird?"

Andy merely shook his head as he had become accustomed to my joy in the simple things in life, while Owen sat there, with a confused look on his face (yes, rear view mirrors do show backseat reactions. A good lesson to anyone who is going into car sales). As I heard the silence become deafening, I continued, in a disheartened tone, "No? No one? Just me... oh..."

Feeling a little heartbroken that no one else was nearly as excited as I was (AKA: nerdy), I quickly decided that this car wasn't for me. If I was going to buy a car from someone, it was to be from a dealer that understood, or at least pretended to understand, my sense of humour.

Which I eventually did in finding the perfect Lancer (blue with four doors), now proudly named Prancer.

BATMAN - The True Identity

I used to live near the cutest breakfast place. Every morning on my way to work, I would walk past this restaurant, staring in their huge front window at the people sitting in the booths, longing for their delicious breakfast.

My boss at the time, Bruce, also loved this joint. So much so, that he would eat there practically every weekday morning, dining with clients as they discussed business. More often than not, I would be beginning my healthy walk to work and see him schmoozing away through the big window.

One morning, I noticed Bruce sitting in the window with a client of ours. It was at this moment I had an epiphany - Bruce was dining with our client, Wayne. Bruce and Wayne were eating breakfast together...Bruce and Wayne...Bruce and Wayne. That's when it hit me: **BRUCE WAYNE!!!** HOLY SMOKES!

BATMAN!!!

Having to stop on the sidewalk, I stared, slack-jawed, and unable to move with my realization. Batman was not one individual! There was simply no way that one man could ever combat so much crime. Batman was actually the combination of 2 men, whose first names were Bruce and Wayne! The real "Batman" was sitting in front of me, here in Calgary, eating breakfast, and most likely refuelling after a long night of crime fighting.

Obviously, comic books had to condense this hero into one man since "Batmen" just didn't have the same ring to it, nor the same extraordinary feel of "Batman."

Once I made this discovery, I looked at my boss and client in a new way. I didn't see them as mere businessmen, but heroes with tortured pasts. I never let them know that I knew there secret, but was much more understanding when Bruce had to suddenly leave the office for a "meeting."

Eventually, the burden of knowing Batman's identity became too great a weight for me. This is why I'm sharing this secret with you. However, I'm just going to ask that you please keep Batman's true identity a secret.

Pull the Furby

When I was in Grade 12, I had a spare period at the end of every second day, meaning no class to take. While I could have used the free time to study or practice singing, I had three other friends with this same spare. Each spare we would head over to Second Cup or McDonald's and chat away the hour.

Throughout the year, each gal began dating a fella. Each gal, except for me, the Late Bloomer of the group. This lead to many conversations about boyfriend issues (and giggles), all of which I was unable to add any insight to.

To get to our places of conversations, we would never walk. Rather, we ended up taking off in my 1988 Oldsmobile - the Funk Mobile - and would go to McDonald's for their super salty fries. One day, Chelsea, ordered a Happy Meal and eagerly opened up her package to see what her Happy Meal toy was. Much to her delight she got a vibrating Furby; one where you pulled its tail and it would vibrate - very fun and incredibly entertaining.

When we got back to my car, Chelsea pulled out the Furby and hung it from my rear-view mirror saying, "Since you're the only one who doesn't have a boyfriend, I am giving you the vibrating Furby. He can be your boyfriend!"

While we all giggled at the time, a wee part of me was a little sad thinking "this is my boyfriend."

That is...until all three gals broke up with their boyfriends and I still had my vibrating Furby.

Now, over 15 years later, my Furby has changed cars with me (from the Funk Mobile, to Rozie the Cavalier, and now Prancer the Lancer) and still vibrates when I pull its...tail. This has been the longest, and by far the most reliable and compatible relationship that I have ever had!

Quiet, always there when I need him, and able to make me laugh when I need it most; there is much to be said for this type of relationship. The relationship between a woman and her *ahem* vibrating Furby is not something that can be broken, not even from overuse.

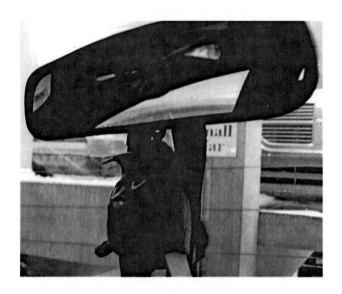

Sexy Dancing and an 18 Year Old

When I first started getting back into performing, one of the first musicals I was in was *Chess*. Being tall and somewhat slim, I was cast as a sexy, dancing prostitute.

However, since I'm quite the geeky and quirky individual, "sexy prostitute" was a big challenge. What made it worse, was that I had to dance quite seductively with someone, let's call him Junior, who was 10 years my junior (not even in my half my age +7 rule!). Every time we practiced this scene, Junior refused to look me in the eye. The only good part about this is that he was freshly 18...so at least the "sexy" wasn't illegal.

At one point during a dance rehearsal, the choreographer told Junior and me that we had to dance a bit sexier since we looked as though we had space for the Holy Ghost to fit between us. His exact words were, "dance as though you are grinding up on stage." I blushed, Junior giggled.

As I was trying to add more sexy, Junior did the "white man's" dance; the one with a simple step touch with the feet and index fingers point upwards in the air.

Needless to say, I was a bit discouraged at my first attempt to be a sexy cougar.

To see how my cougar approach could be improved, I summoned up all my courage and asked Junior if he was ok with the sexy dancing since it seemed a wee bit uncomfortable.

Junior ever so slowly turned his head, looking me straight in the eye for the first time since we started rehearsals three months before and ever so subtly, eagerly nodded his head and breathed out, "Yeah. My friends at work make fun of me for doing musical theatre...but it's awesome being a straight, single male doing this!"

Then, everything from then on in changed. He realized that this geeky cougar wanted him to be a bit more handsy, helping to add a bit more believable "sexiness" to the prostitute dance. He stopped the toe tapping and finger waived and grabbed me from there on out.

It was at that point that I thought that I could become a cougar, almost deciding to revise my half my age +7 rule thinking that every late twenties something woman should have a fresh 18-year-old crossed off their bucket list.

Almost, but not quite.

Pun Lessons: Punny for a Reason

- The most mundane activities in life can often be the ones that bring the most giggles. What giggles are you missing out on within the mundane?
- You're meant to have people in your life that understand – or at least don't look down upon – your humour. If they do look down upon you, they're not meant to be there.
- 5 seconds of courage is all it takes to change a situation.

A Family Built on Laughs

There is nothing funnier than a person's family...particularly when there's a healthy combination of prim and proper and subtle wit.

Why Grandmother, What a Potty Mouth You Have!

When I was in university, there was a course called "Human Sexuality." Every semester, including the spring and summer sessions, this class would fill up as soon as registration opened, particularly since it was said to have the most interesting guest speakers from sex therapists to sex shop owners. Among university students who were horny...ahem, thirsty for knowledge...this was *the* course to take.

I was one of the fortunate students, lucky enough to get into a spring session of this course. I say this in complete honesty: it was by far one of the most interesting classes I have ever taken, and not just because of all the knowledge I gained. Of course, having lived at home during university, this course provided much amusement for Mom when I would study at her kitchen table, especially since my textbook had many an illustration, demonstrating certain "topics."

A sampling of my mom's comments from her peanut gallery:

- "Why is she sucking his thumb? Oh my...that's not his thumb! What are you reading at my table?!"
- "Well, that's all I've ever found use for [the clit]."
- "You don't want me to join you as a guest when the presenter's the owner of a sex shop? Why"

After eight weeks of classroom fun, a midterm and a final, the grades were in and I was at the top of the class – there was some intense studying after each new lesson. I told my mom this and she was so pleased that she called up my prim and proper Grandmother to tell her the news of my grades.

Ecstatically, my Grandmother asked to speak to me, where our conversation took a turn I did not expect:

Me: Hi Grandmother. How are you?

GM: I am absolutely thrilled for you and your marks. I am so proud - I'm speechless.

*Note this "speechless" was a feat unto itself as Grandmother had never been one at a loss for words.

Me: Oh my! Thank you.

Quickly finding her voice again – speechless didn't last very long – she went right into her next thought.

GM: Now, tell me dear...what was your mark on the "Oral" portion of the test? *holding her giggles as she knew full well what she meant by "Oral"*

Me: Umm. *Silence.* Here's my mom again.

As my mom took the phone, she sat quietly as a twinkle began to form in her eyes. Suddenly, she burst into laughter as my Grandmother disclosed what she had said to me, while I sat there disturbed by having heard words I never wanted to have said to me by my Grandmother.

Looking back, I suppose that I shouldn't have been as shocked by this statement as I was at the time. My Grandmother was always throwing out these random one-liners that would leave the family stunned into silence. There was just something about being asked by my Grandmother at point blank, about my oral skills.

Passion Party Inquiry

When Andy and I were engaged, the two of us, along with my parents went to the Bridal Expo.

Being overwhelmed by all the wedding booths and people calling you into their booth, trying to become a part of your "big day," my mom and I somehow meandered over to the booth that was selling Passion Parties. They weren't nearly as aggressive as other booths, so it felt like a safe space. Andy and my dad went to another booth – one with a picture of piña coladas and margaritas. They had different priorities that day.

I had a quick chat with the gal at the booth about edible panties and the many flavour varieties that they offered. My mom, simply stood beside me with a "just play it cool" look on her face.

After filling in the raffle form for their giveaway, my mom and I made our way over to the fellas. As we grabbed our own drinks to catch up to the gents, my mom leaned in, and said, "One day, you'll have to explain just what a Passion Party is to me and your father."

Being a bit startled by this statement, considering the edible panties and body chocolate that was being given away, I looked at my mom with a horrified expression.

I immediately, responded, "Umm…no. I think that it's best if you Google what a Passion Party is. Under no circumstance do I want to be responsible for explaining what they are to my parents."

To my knowledge, my mom still as yet to do her research. To my knowledge, of course…

Duct Taping a Friendship

It's not often that you can pinpoint the moment you became good friends with someone, but with my friend Cindy, we know the exact date and time.

Cindy and I met when we were both cast in the musical *Chess* with a local theatre company. The moment where we knew our friendship was solidified happened opening night of the show.

With the musical taking place in the 1980s, most of our costumes were found at used clothing stores. The costume I was given happened to be a very tight pencil skirt – still with all the original threading.

The set itself, while grand, was incredibly awkward, one where you had to contort your body into flexible yoga stances to unlock the locks and then, as they do with Strong Man competitions, use your bulging thigh muscles to manoeuvre the 100 – 300 lbs of solid wood and steel into a new position. Once in position, you took a deep breath and used the remainder of your strength to relock the platforms.

Of course, these changes all had to be done in costume. Remember, I had on a tight skirt with 30+-year-old thread. Bending, flexing, and breathing were not easily done.

On opening night, during a scene change where I had to crouch down and work with the locks, my skirt suddenly split open...all the way up the back, letting a cool rush of air race along my tuckus. The thread simply disintegrated as it wasn't used to the force my rear, contorted in downward dog, was placing on it. As the brisk air started to chill my backside, I quickly finished the set change and ran backstage, realizing that I had to go right back on stage in a matter of seconds.

Backstage, I turned to my director and said "Greg! Greg! My skirt has just split all the way up the back!" His eyes opened wide in surprise as he responded, "It's ok, you just have to go sing this one song and your back won't be to the audience. We'll fix your skirt right after."

I trotted on stage, began to sing with the chorus as the air-conditioned stage swayed the back pieces of my now open skirt, when, halfway through the song I realized that I had to turn around and walk off stage, baring my pasty white rear to a sold out audience. All I could do was complete my exit as staged and hope that no one was looking as this chorus gal.

As soon as I was off stage I found some duct tape and asked Cindy to help me. Without hesitation, she quickly put her hand up the back of my skirt, and duct taped like a pro! I breathed out a sigh of relief, so the skirt, with no thread, allowed my to comfortably in and exhale. With everything was taped in place, we finished off the show.

While Cindy was quick to help me with the duct tape, she wasn't able to look me in the eye for the rest of the run. However, conversation certainly didn't cease as she recognized that I was a kindred spirit in the World of Awkward.

Later that night, I found out that a couple of friends were in the audience as they waited around after the show. While chatting with them, one friend mentioned that she saw my skirt split and saw my super white granny panties as I tried to stealthily get off stage. I looked at her in sheer horror, squealing, "I'm not wearing white granny panties. I'm wearing a hot pink thong. You totally saw my bum!" Naturally, we burst out laughing at just how white my Canadian bum was. Secretly, I was crying inside, kicking myself for thinking that a hot pink thong was an appropriate undergarment to perform in, even if it wicked the sweat away.

I quickly told Cindy about my white exposure and she responded with, "yeah...it was a little blinding back there as I was putting on the duct tape. Quite up close and personal, so I guess we're just going to have to be really good friends now."

Needless to say that Cindy and I have pretty much been taped together ever since the skirt splitting incident. After all, with someone who is that talented with duct tape, you pretty much don't ever want to turn her into an enemy. Who knows what other uses she might put her duct taping skills towards?

Meeting the Parents

The first time I went to pick d Cindy up from her home, she was still living with her folks, sister and family cat. While at the time, we had been friends for a year, I had not yet met her parents. That said, her dad is an avid tomato grower and had sent many a tomato with Cindy for me when we hung out. To this day, his tomatoes are some of the most delicious I have ever tasted and I would always send many a thank you home with her.

As I pulled up to Cindy's house, I wasn't too sure what to expect, as I had never been there before. As I walked up to her front door, she greeted me with a big "Hello! I just have to put on my shoes! Come on in." I walked in and her dad eagerly came to the front hall to meet the gal who had been eating his delicious tomatoes. Once he was in the front foyer, Cindy's sister joined, then her mom and finally her cat. They all stood there, extremely excited, watching Cindy and I getting ready to leave.

Having never experienced this amount of friendliness from a friend's family before, I was a little uncertain with what was going on. The only time that I had ever seen this enthusiasm was watching graduation episodes of sitcoms where the gal walks down the stairs as the fella is waiting with her corsage and her entire family is there, ready to capture the moment on camera.

To try and break, or augment, the obvious awkwardness of the situation, Cindy's sister picked up the cat and said, "You know that every single living thing is in this tiny front hall, right?" We all had a good chuckle, but Cindy and I quickly left.

As we walked to my car, Cindy and I looked at one another and started laughing. I finally said, "Is it just me or did that feel like I was picking you up for a prom? Did we just cross from friends into a relationship without either of us knowing?"

Since both Cindy and I had been single for some time, navigating the waters of dating men in Calgary, we took a quick minute to decide that maybe this possible new relationship would be easier. However, we realized that we just like the fellas too much; friendship was all that we could have if we truly wanted all our needs meet in a romantic way.

Looking back, I believe that this incident sufficiently prepared me to handle the meet and greet of Andy's family...just with a dog, not a cat.

A Fish Named Gert

Before meeting Andy, I made the decision to throw myself into a fairly committed relationship with a betta fish named Gert. From day one, Gert and I got along swimmingly.

During my darkest of days, Gert was always there for a laugh, was incredibly smart, recognized me (at feeding time anyways), and was always the champion during our daily staring competitions.

When Gert was in my life, Cindy decided to let me know that Gert was really the only fish that she ever liked, simply because he was so awesome, friendly, and super colourful. Plus, she didn't have to feed him or clean his tank, so was less likely to kill him, unlike the other fish she used to be responsible for (this is Cindy's story, not mine to tell. I don't want to say anything incriminating that would damage Cindy's reputation).

Cindy admitted, quite proudly, that she tried to describe him to her sister, but just couldn't quite capture his true essence. They even went to the pet store, but were unable to find another betta that resembled my Gert. So, when Cindy admitted her love of Gert to me, I volunteered my excellent drawing skills to do a portrait of him for Cindy to show her family.

In a matter of minutes, I completed Gert's portrait and sent it home with Cindy, eager to hear her family's thoughts about my wonderful Gert. When she got home, everyone was asleep, so she left the picture on the kitchen table with a note saying that I had drawn this picture of Gert for them.

The next morning, Cindy sleepily wandered into the kitchen only to find Gert's picture hanging on the fridge, just like parents do for their children's art work in elementary school.

Her mom and dad were sitting at the table eating breakfast when Cindy asked them what they thought of my drawing. Cindy's mom paused, choosing her words wisely. "Well, Gert certainly has a lot of...personality." To which her dad replied with a confused tone, "That's a fish? I thought it was a gay seal!"

Clearly, my drawing abilities aren't nearly at the level that I thought they were.

My First Swear Word

Overall, I often come across as quite the reserved individual, reminding people of more simple times when I use words such as, "gosh," "golly," and, "swell." I say these so often that I don't even realize that I say them anymore, only to have fun poked at me when I do say them.

This said, I do have these Jekyll and Hyde moments, particularly when driving. My choice of words changes drastically if I don't slowly count to 10 or practice my yoga breathing. If another car cuts me off and doesn't give me a thank you wave, my blood begins to boil, my veins begin to pop out of my biceps, and sometimes, I will turn purple in colour. Then, when I am swollen, I start swearing up a storm and go from Miss Manners to Road Rage Queen! This has led to many a laugh for my friends when they witness this. They are surprised when they hear the words that I am able to string together* and laughter is their only coping mechanism in managing the fear that is growing within them.

Then, just like that, I'm back to my "golly gosh" ways.

Through hours upon hours of long counselling sessions focused on this very topic of Jekyll and Hyde, I think I have finally been able to pinpoint where my road rage swearing comes from; A memory that I don't quite remember, but one that has been permanently ingrained on my mother's brain.

My mother tells me this is where my rage swears began:

When I was two, my family and I went out to an Italian restaurant for a delicious dinner. As I always had a love of spaghetti, my Mom ordered me the kid-sized portion and we all eagerly awaited our meal.

Finally after hours or 15 minutes – when you're two, your time is similar to that of a puppy, 1 minute apart equals a lifetime of waiting – the waitress came to our table, holding plates of food and smiling away. As she set my spaghetti in front of me, a strand covered in sauce slipped off the side of the plate. I, in my wee infant voice, squeaked out "God Dammit!"

The waitress looked at me, then to my parents in pure shock, deciding if she should laugh, give a sympathetic smile to my parents, or give a condescending look that these adults would deign to bring a Satan's spawn to a restaurant. She settled on awkward laugh. My Mom looked beyond horrified that her normally giggling, chubby baby was not just swearing, but swearing in public! As my Mom processed the horror of her embarrassment, my Dad leaned back in his chair, smiling as he never had before, feeling a sense of pride that only a father could feel as he witnessed his child step into verbal independence.

Based on these reactions, it quickly became clear whom I learned the word from.

They say that it is our early experiences that shape us as adults. With starting to swear at such a young age, it's no wonder why I am able to bring out the road rage when someone releases my inner Hulk when driving.

*I cannot write down the things I say because 1) I don't remember what I spurt out, going into a trancelike state, and 2) apparently what I say not very friendly.

My Parents' Birth Control

While I try to avoid "Parent Sex" conversations, I have been involved in a few with my Mom, much to my utter horror. During these conversations, my belief that my parents are asexual beings, simply not interested in sex, is shaken to its very core. However, I still choose to believe that 1) my birth was merely a blessing by a Baby-Giving Stork, and / or 2) I was a test-tube baby.

What's important to know is that my parents married very young (ages 20 and 21), then waited 12 years prior to having my sister and then three more to have me. They travelled the world, built careers, and grew up together before settling down in the early thirties to start a family.

When I was in my early twenties, my Mom and I somehow started talking about birth control. While I don't quite remember how we landed on the topic, I do know that we had the conversation when I was my taking a Human Sexuality class at university, where I would come home after every session with loads of new information, ready to share with my asexual mother.

During one of my class retellings, my Mom mentioned that she did not really like being on the birth control pill; that it gave her some side effects she wasn't overly fond of. Curious about why my non-sex participating Mom would be on birth control, I asked when was she actually on it since I don't remember this and after I was born no more babies were arrived.

My Mom kindly replied to me, "During the '70s. Your father and I had to use something to not get pregnant before having a family. What did you think we did?"

At this point, my thoughts and beliefs were being unnecessarily challenged and I was grasping so strongly to my stork and / or test-tube theory that I yelled out, "I don't know. ABSTAIN!!"

I got the "Mother Look" like I've never gotten before. The one that said, "Lindsay, don't be stupid." She then rolled her eyes, let out an exasperated breath that her daughter was that naïve, or ignorant, or stupidly blinded by her faith, and turned around to walk away.

It's been well over a decade since we had this challenge of beliefs, and I have done my best to steer clear of these conversations with my mother, bringing up topics of grilled cheese sandwiches and road rage to divert our attention at all costs. After all, there are just some beliefs that should never be challenged because of the comfort they provide.

A Father's Advice

The first boyfriend I ever brought home for Sunday night family dinner was Shane. At the time we had been dating for five months at the time.

Everything seemed to be going well - conversation flowed easily, jokes were being made, and I'm pretty sure my Dad was enjoying having another male presence in the house after years of female domination. Heck, even our family rabbits were female. So much estrogen needed some balancing for my Dad.

Over the years it became apparent that I could be a little absent-minded and, as a result, would often have many a klutz moment, tripping over flat floors and walking into walls that weren't jutting out in any fashion. However, it was during this Sunday dinner that my father gave Shane and I some unexpected advice due to my clumsy absent-mind.

At the end of dinner, I was about to get up to clear the dirty dishes off the table. I began to stand up without realizing that my legs were still crossed. Naturally, I began to tumble backwards, since crossed legs don't make for easy standing. As I stumbled back down to my bum, I giggled out, "Oops, I forgot to uncross my legs."

My Dad looked at Shane, then right back at me, and without any hesitation, but a slight chuckle responds, "Well, let's just hope they stay crossed." I laughed while rolling my eyes and saying "Oh, Dad!" Thinking Shane would have a similar reaction, I looked at him to share in the laughter. I was wrong. Rather than humour, I saw pure mortification across his face. A look of, "Oh God...I swear, I've never touched her. Not once. Please don't kill me, sir!"

While my Dad still chuckled away, I got up – legs uncrossed – and took the dishes away. Shane followed right on my heels, grabbing the salt and pepper shaker so he looked like he too was clearing the table and not just running away.

Fortunately, my Dad never brought the comment up again, nor did Shane. That said, Shane did keep his distance over the next few weeks, only holding my hand from time to time until my Dad's comment faded from his memory.

Of course, my father's comment definitely taught me a few lessons that, to this day, have remained forefront in my mind:

1. Always uncross your legs when you need to get up from the table,
2. Warn your boyfriend that your Dad may make some unsightly comments about keeping one's legs permanently crossed, and
3. Make sure you and your boyfriend have both perfected the "oh don't be silly" face so that no one suspects the truth!

Winter Solstice Time

After living in Alberta for 28 years, my parents decided to retire to British Columbia where my Dad could cycle all year round without having to battle the brutal cold of winter.

One Christmas holiday, I arrived early in the morning where my Dad very kindly picked me up at the airport. When I say early, I mean pre-coffee early. Coming from a home of coffee drinkers, this meant that my Dad wasn't quite fully awake yet.

On the drive back to my parents' house, our conversation went like this:

Dad: Guess What?!

Me: Chicken butt...hee hee

Dad: No. Guess what happens in a few days?

Me: Umm...Christmas?

Dad: Well, yes, but no. The days will start to get longer!! *With the excitement of a pre-schooler in his voice and a twinkle in his eye*

Me: Hahahaha. I love how excited you get about longer days and sunlight. *Quietly thinking to myself: clearly my Dad is not a vampire. Phew!*

Dad: Well...it's exciting. Days getting longer is a great, great thing!

Seeing my Dad with the enthusiasm of a five year old at Christmas time just brought the giggles to my heart. I love that I even though we don't have Christmas at the home I grew up in, that I still get to go "home" to celebrate the longer days and return of sunshine with my Dad.

Earlobe Deception Incident

To say my parents are conservative when it comes to clothing, tattoos, and body piercings is quite the understatement. Anything other than having one hole punched into your earlobe is simply ruining the "beautiful body you were born with" as my Dad likes to say anytime tattoos or extra piercings are mentioned.

Fortunately, they agreed that my sister and I could get ONE set of ear piercings under specific rules. Namely, we had to be 10 before we could get them.

My sister, being older, naturally got her ears done first. I remember being so jealous of the new jewels that glistened from her ears. However, a mere 35 months later, my parents took pity on me. Three weeks before my 10th birthday, my mom surprised me and took me to get my ears pierced so they would be all pretty when my family went to see *Les Miserables*. I remember choosing green emeralds as my studs to bring a pop of colour.

With my studs picked out, the gal assigned to my ear piercing sat me down, prepped my ear, and brought the gun up to my ear. Then, she swore...a lot. Apparently, I had the fattest earlobes she had ever experienced and the studs just weren't going through on the first shot. A trooper to sit through pain, there were a few more shots through my ear and finally I had my ears pierced, along with new words to add to my vocabulary.

For the next five years, I was in heaven with my earrings.

Then I turned 15. As I was about to enter Grade 10, I kept hinting to my Mom that I would like to get a second hole in my ears so I would feel more mature. Like a woman, not a teenager. Finally, she caved and went with me to get my second earring hole done a couple weeks before I started High School. I was so ecstatic. I thought my Mom was growing as an individual and becoming so cool. I also thought this second hole would change my life and I would no longer be the extreme geek that I was in Junior High; that I would now become one of the "cool kids" in High School since I had not one, but 2 sets of earrings. That's how it worked, right?

No such luck. While I did love my earring holes, there just seemed to be something missing. Apparently, earrings have nothing to do with how "cool" you were. Who knew?

Yet, one April afternoon of my Grade 10 year, my friend, Trish, and I were wondering through the mall and came across Claire's, the jewellery store that also pierces ears. With a little (and I mean little) encouragement from Trish, I quickly got a third hole done in both ears, feeling very mature that I had made this decision all on my own.

At the time I had fairly short hair and knew that my newly pierced ears would not be something I could hide. "But," I thought to myself, "my Mom was so cool with the second hole, she'll have no problem with a third. Of course, because she's so cool, I'll just keep this to myself and let her discover them on her own...just in case."

To my astonishment, my Mom didn't notice my third hole for over a week. When she did, we were sitting in the computer room, me on the floor sorting through some photos, my mom on the chair at her computer. When she looked up and kept a strong gaze on the sides of my head. Then we had words:

Mom: What's that?

Me: What?

Mom: In your ears?

Me: *silence...and a reddening face*

Mom: Did you get your ears pierced again? *hint of disappointed anger in her voice*

Me: *squeak* Yes

Mom: How could you deceive me like this? *daggers shooting out of eyes*

Me: I didn't *an ashamed and uncomfortable, yet highly cheeky smile creeping across my face*

Mom: Umm hmm *Mom Look of dark coals, disappointment seeping out of her head and enveloping my entire soul, a slight cock of her left eyebrow, and the corners of her mouth turned down, then dead silence*

It is this disappointment that withers one's belief that they didn't do anything wrong. The disappointment that doesn't need words or even a punishment since the "Mom Look" is punishment enough. No raising of the voice, just a look. When you get the look, the discussion has finished forever. To this very day nearly two decades later, we still haven't discussed my Earlobe Deception.

Every now and then I'll broach the subject with my Mom saying, "Well, at least I only wear barely-there studs." To which I simply get her "Mom Look" that would keep even the most harmful of murderers from doing any wrong, and the topic is finished.

I may try having this conversation again when I'm 55, but we'll see.

I Love My Calendar Girls

Growing up my Mom and I would go on mother / daughter movie dates. It was a great way to spend some quality time together while seeing some pretty awesome movies that neither my Dad nor sister wanted to see.

One movie date stands out as it wasn't about the movie or the previews that made it special, but the audience in the theatre. This was when we went to see Calendar Girls, a movie about several middle age women who pose nude for a calendar to raise funds for a new sofa at the hospital where one of the women's husbands stayed during his cancer treatment. This was a movie that both my mom and I wanted to see, but my Dad wasn't so sure since advertisements geared it toward middle age+ women as the key demographic. Thus, a mother / daughter date it was.

We got to the theatre early and began to enjoy munching on our popcorn. While sitting and chatting with each other, we noticed there were three older gentlemen sitting in the row in front of us, just to the left of our seats. Among a theatre full of gaggles of women, these three definitely stood out.

My Mom leaned over to me and cheekily said, "I wonder what drew they're interest here?"

As we both knew that the ladies in the film posed nude for the calendar, I quietly whispered back to her, "Maybe it's their version of porn?"

My mom and I chuckled as silently as we could, but there were definitely some peeps that escaped.

This date was by far one of the best ones my Mom and I ever had.

Lessons on Introducing the Boyfriend

Since my parents do not live in the same province as me, it is rare that they met anyone I dated throughout my twenties. However, when Andy and I first started dating, my parents were going for a ski weekend in Lake Louise. As Andy and I had been dating for about four months at the time, we thought it would be fun to meet in Banff for lunch, as well as a parent / boyfriend introduction.

As Andy and I drove to Banff, I reviewed my **"Meet the Parents"** checklist to make sure that all our bases were covered and the meeting would go smoothly.

1. Tell your boyfriend your parents' names. Check!
2. Cover topics of conversation that can be discussed. Check!

> "How about your local sports team?"
> "How was your day on the slopes?"

3. Approve boyfriend's outfit. Check!
4. Tell boyfriend your parents' ages. Check!
5. Remind boyfriend that age 65 is not old...FAIL!

I had told my boyfriend that both my parents are 65, very active and enjoying their lives to the fullest right now. Not only that, but they don't look a day over 50 (lucky future me!).

We met at the Maple Leaf Grill, introductions went easily, and we all sat down, ready to eat some lunch. Halfway through the lunch, the conversation turned to the topic about one of Andy's uncles and his then current fight against throat cancer.

My Dad asked if Andy's uncle was fairly young (since Andy's parents were in their early 50s at the time), to which Andy replied, "No, he's old. I think he's 65."

I closed my eyes and slowly shook my head, while my parents caught each other's eyes, both with a twinkle of humour in glistening through as they started to chuckle.

I leaned over and said to Andy, "65's not old." Poor Andy, realizing what he had said, quickly said, "Or maybe my uncle's 75...I can't remember."

Thankfully my parents both have a good sense of humour and simply laughed, recognizing that Andy had some parent meeting jitters still. From there, the conversation quickly moved to good ski hills.

After this meeting, I decided that I may need to revise my **"Meet the Parent's Checklist"** to pass along to future generations, with a disclaimer saying that each and every step must be followed to avoid accidentally insulting the significant other's family.

When the Red Robin Comes Bopping Along

Growing up I was a pretty superstitious. I never stepped on a crack for fear that I would break my mother's back and I always said "God Bless You" after someone sneezed, lest the devil escaped from them. And the stack of pennies that I have at home to this day...well, they were supposed to bring me loads of good luck when I found them laying on the ground! Because of my superstition, I believed that there were omens all around.

When I was 15, my sister, Robin, went to university on the other side of the country. It was the first time in our lives that we were separated for more than a week at a time and I was surprisingly sad and lonely when she left. I say surprisingly because we weren't all that close when we were young. I think my protective mode of my sister kicked in since I couldn't see her every day.

One evening a few weeks after she had left, I went upstairs to my bedroom and saw an odd shape lying on the roof outside of my window. Dark, small, and unmoving, I grew curious as I had never seen this shape before. Tentatively, I walked over, coming across a sight that disturbed me to my core.

Right outside of my window, lying right in front of my teenage eyes, was a dead bird. Not just any bird, but a dead robin red breast. I became distraught, thinking that this was the most negative of omens ever. Something bad must be about to happen to my one and only sister! To MY ROBIN! Without thinking, I ran downstairs to the living room where my parents where relaxing after a long day at work. With tears streaming down my face, snot pouring out of my eyes, I croaked out that Robin was going to die.

Once I caught my breath, I told them that there was a dead robin outside my window. My Mom, ever so gently, said that a robin must have flown into my closed bedroom window and died. My Dad, on the other hand, rolled his eyes, got out of his reading chair, and went upstairs to collect the bird (and throw it in the trash I'm guessing…where dead animals and fish went, I never asked). While he did this, my Mom continued to try and comfort me, but was holding in some chuckles as she told me Robin wasn't going to die. She was doing just fine and will live a long, long life. It was just an accident that this bird flew into my window.

I called Robin the next day (after all – she was a few hours ahead of us, so I didn't want to wake her) to make sure that she was, in fact, ok and that she was to be careful wherever she went. Again, you could tell there were some giggles and eye rolls coming from the other end of the phone in the fashion that only an older sister could make. The tone of "don't be so silly my younger, less wiser sibling."

As the days, weeks, months, even years went on, Robin is still a-ok (*knock on wood*), causing my superstitious side to begin dwindling.

While my superstitious beliefs have calmed down, the truth is that I really only prefer to see robin red breasts singing their song or eating the early worm.

But, I still wonder to this day, what would have happened if the bird had been a Blue Jay?

Learning to Compromise One Burger at a Time

When Andy and I decided to move in together, we had only been dating for six months. While six months determined that we really loved one another, it certainly wasn't enough to know all of our living habits inside and out. That can only come when you are truly in each other's space.

The first few weeks were a truly a big adjustment. While we had both lived with significant others in the past, we both still had a lot to learn about living with the opposite sex. For me, there were five key areas where I was shocked and had to lower any dream fantasy that I was living with someone who had the exact same living habits as myself.

1. **Clothes**
   Andy has a preference for dropping his work overalls the moment he walks in the door, right smack dab in the middle of the living room...without concern for the wide-open windows facing the street. From there, he proceeds to walk around in his skivvies the rest of the evening. It isn't until the following morning when he walks down to the living room and pulls his overalls back on...in front of the window.

   For me, I am a firm believer in taking your clothes off in the bedroom (most of the time...there are always exceptions to this rule of course) and promptly putting them in the hamper. I've since learned to do a quick run around the house once a week to make sure I've picked up all of Andy's clothes prior to starting the laundry.

2. **Bed**
   Since I was old enough to make my own bed, I've made it every single morning the moment I jump up. Yes, this is a bit anal, but it gives me a kick in the butt to start the day and not crawl back in for some more zzz's. Andy,

like many a fella, doesn't like to make the bed...ever. This was a big frustration at first, but since he gets up a 5:00 am, I've learned to let this go. I'd really rather he not make the bed while I'm still sleeping in it.

3. **Phone Chats**

   I like to chat on the phone for long periods of time with my friends, mom and sister (all whom live in other cities). Andy likes to dance in front of me while I'm trying to chat, usually as he's dropping his pants. I get distracted and am never fully caught up with the other person on the phone due to the "sexy" dancing that is happening in front of me.

4. **Bodily Music**

   Andy is a trophy winning farter. I am the queen of all ye who burps. Neither of us supports the other's body noise, each indicating how unattractive and unsexy it is. Yet, we still do them. This is the only music we've ever made together.

5. **Food**

   Andy is strictly a meat, potatoes, and corn guy. I like my veggies and healthy meals. As such, I try to sneak healthiness into our dinners as much as possible. This is where we started to go awry on our living together compromises...

Since I work from home, I am often the one who starts making dinner. Usually, I try to make a dish one night that Andy likes (some form of red meat, accompanied by corn and potatoes), the next night I make one that I prefer and so on. However, a couple nights in a row, I had some zucchini and orange peppers that needed to be used up.

The first night I thought, "I know! I'll make pasta and in the pasta sauce I can add the veggies that need to be used.

Brilliant! Andy won't even taste them. And since there won't be any onions (a big no-no in any food, on any night – this goes for both of us), he won't have anything to complain about. Awesome!"

The outcome: the pasta sauce went off without a hitch!

The next day, I was scouring the fridge and freezer trying to decide what to make for dinner. I found a package of ground beef, hamburger buns, and still more zucchini and peppers (I'm pretty sure there was a sale at the grocery store that week). I remembered seeing a recipe for meatloaf hamburgers requiring all these ingredients. The wannabe chef in me was inspired and I went to work, making burgers from scratch, containing super healthy veggies chopped up into tiny bits. Surely, Andy would never notice the veggies and since he agreed to my "let's have burgers for dinner" text, I figured this would be a delightful surprise.

Oops.

When Andy saw the uncooked burgers formed into patties, he flipped, telling me that we had enough veggies the night before and that I needed to compromise a little more on the food. Apparently not everyone likes having veggies all the time and that we had frozen burgers in the freezer, left over from his "Men's Camping Trip" the weekend before and that no one should never, ever mess with a man's burger.

After a half hour argument about the burgers, although I'm certain there was more than just the burgers that we had to discuss as we got to know what living with someone was like, Andy went and started to barbecue the patties I had made. He realized that since I was the one who planned the dinner and acted upon making it, that he should just go and cook them up. Burgers with veggies in them would be better than no dinner at all as that was the other option I presented.

After 5 minutes of him grilling, all I heard was swearing coming from our balcony. The burgers were falling apart, one by one, without being touched. They were simply going limp on the grill, falling between the spaces and into the fire.

As I saw the red starting to come up Andy's neck, I quickly said, "Forget about them then. I'll pull the frozen ones out and we can use those." However, the frozen burgers had been sneakily super glued together by the packaging company. I quickly tried to pry them apart in an unsuccessful battle of ice versus human fingers. Hearing my struggle, Andy came over and tried to use his tradesman fingers...with no luck.

We decided that maybe if we run them under warm water, they'll come apart, much like the lid of a jar. However, we forgot that burgers and glass jars are not the same consistency. Science was not going to be on our side this night as the warm water turned the burgers into pink mush. Pink mush that still refused to un-stick from one another.

After a few more minutes of swearing, Andy quietly went upstairs to my office. I thought he was just going to have a moment to calm down, then we would figure out what cheese and crackers we would like for dinner since it was now 8:30 pm.

Over the next hour I let him be until I heard a knock on our door at 9:30. Andy came running downstairs, pushing me out of the way to open the door. The smell of Swiss Chalet instantly hit my nose as he greeted the delivery man.

With two-quarter chicken dinners (white meat only) in hand, Andy went into the kitchen and plated our dinner. We quickly dug right in. After our first few bites, Andy looked at me and sheepishly said, "Wow, these are the best burgers I've ever had in my life."

Bursting out laughing, I knew we would be alright.

Of course, I did learn a huge lesson that day about living with a boy:

Never try to make a man's meat "fancy" by sneaking in veggies.

Converting...How Does it Really Work?

I always believed that I was special because my Dad's mom (my Granny) and I shared the same birthday. In June of 2010, she passed away unexpectedly, even though she was 92. Knowing we wouldn't have our special birthday phone call that year (or the rest of my years), I was in no mood to actually celebrate our birthday that year, as it was just a couple months after her passing.

Fortunately for me, my friend, Lisa, was going to Vancouver Pride that year, which subsequently was happening on the long weekend of my birthday. Knowing I didn't really want to celebrate my birthday, she invited me along, and I jumped at the chance to go. A weekend celebrating love in all its forms - how could I say no, and what better distraction could there be?

Every year, my Grandmother (my Mom's mother) would send me a lovely birthday card, filled with lots of love and joy. This year was no different. She again sent me a beautiful card, but this time with a very caring and heartfelt note talking about my Granny and how she was such a special lady. Just as I started to tear up, she suddenly switched tones in the middle of her letter, saying:

Your mother told me of your trip to Vancouver for the "Gay Pride" Parade. It will be a startling change - let me know if you get converted.

Knowing my 96 year old, wit-wielding Grandmother, I could hear the tongue and cheek tone she was writing that sentence with and I burst out laughing, promptly starting to write a thank you note to her.

With the same tongue and cheek tone, my response was simple (after all, I'm pretty sure I got my wit from her):

Don't worry, Grandmother. I'm pretty sure that I won't come back converted. From what I understand, that's not how it works.

Shortly after she received the card, we had a little chat on the phone, chuckling over her cheekiness.

As this was one of the last cards I ever received from my Grandmother, I am so happy that it had so much of her humour in it, as it makes me smile every time I read it.

Of course, Lisa and I did go to Pride and, wouldn't you know it, we certainly did not come back converted. Looks like I was right!

The Perks of Being a Senior (So I'm Told)

My parents, while biologically are considered seniors, do not live the lifestyle, or have the looks (all natural) of someone considered "senior."

While I'm often hearing about getting older – the aches and pains, loss of hearing (perhaps by choice), memory hiccups, the hot flashes (ladies), earlier and earlier bedtimes and so on - I rarely hear about the truly awesome side of becoming a senior, other then, well...living to be a senior which is a pretty awesome feat unto its own.

The year my Dad turned 65 he was called for Jury Duty. At first, he wasn't exactly thrilled because this duty would certainly cut into his playtime. Then he learnt that by being a "senior" in the eyes of the Canadian Government, he had an extreme advantage. Apparently, when one turns 65 in Canada they have the ability to decline participating in Jury Duty. No reason is needed other than, "I don't want to."

Now, not really wanting to serve Jury Duty, not because he wanted to shirk any "civic responsibility," but because was retired and his jammed-packed schedule just wouldn't allow it. So, my dad chose to say "no" to Jury Duty. As I was chatting about this with him, he put it simply: my Dad served his civic duty throughout his 40+ years of work and was ready to have fun. Finally, at 65, my Dad discovered that it's time to prioritize his *fun* over **duty**.

And, since every time I call my parents they're either out of the house travelling, hiking, or attending some soiree, or at home, but just about to open a bottle of wine for friends who are over, I can say that he is learning quite well.

As for me, having been called for Jury Duty twice before the age of 25, I can honestly say that I cannot wait to turn 65 and be able to say "no" to Jury Duty without requiring a legitimate excuse.

Family Lessons: A Source of Laughter

- Listen to your grandparents' wisdom; it could guide you to finding your own self...or really bad humour.
- Parents are allowed to have sex lives too. *shiver*
- Your family should be a source of support. If not, look to your friends. If you have both supporting you, you're pretty luck.
- It isn't always, "like Mother, like Daughter." It can often be "like Father, like Daughter."
- When moving in with someone, make sure you know how they like their meat.

Uplifted Physicality

To break my own body image issues, learning to laugh at the hilarity of the human body – whether in body function, coordination, or weird hair growth – has become the best way to accept myself. Cellulite on my thighs are simply my legs' way of smiling at the world (when in shorts, of course). How is your unique body something to lovingly smile at?

It's All in the Bangs

For years, I had an amazing short angled bob with perfectly cut bangs.* The long and the short of it – I had an amazing hairdresser with vision! Not to brag, but my hair generated all kinds of compliments from random people on the street, in stores, and even restaurants. To be fair...the compliments were not for me, but for my hair.

At the time of this amazing hairstyle, I lived in an apartment building on a street known throughout Calgary for the night time activity that would take place both day and night á la *Pretty Woman* style. To put it simply, there were a number of regular "workers" just outside my building.

One sunny Saturday afternoon, I was walking down my street and passed two of the regular "workers," one of who happened to be a transvestite. From a distance, she looks like a gorgeous, stacked woman, but up close, you can see that she has a large part "he."

Not expecting any light-hearted afternoon conversation from them, I simply walked by. Out of nowhere, this low, booming voice says to me, "I love your hair! Your bangs are perfect!"*

Incredibly flustered, I turned around and squeaked out "ooooohhhh! Thank you!" Having fantastic hair herself, she did a hair flip, turned back in the direction she was going and kept on strutting. For some strange reason, this compliment of my hairdresser's abilities made me feel like I was walking on Cloud 9.

I then had the biggest hop in my step for the rest of my day. Whenever I feel like I need a wee pick me up, I just remember that story and how this working lady made me feel great!

A haircut truly can change a woman's life.

---

*Please note that the drawing is meant to give an idea of what my hair looked like at the time...in the end it tells a little bit more about my drawing skills...

A Mom, Some Lipstick and the 1950's!

When I was first put on antidepressants, my constant crying stopped suddenly. Thankfully since I was beginning to get parched by all the water my eye sockets had let escape!

However, after not crying for over a month, I began to wonder if I had lost my emotions altogether. After all, I went from feeling absolutely everything all at once to nothing at all – no downs or ups. This worrying was for nothing when I finally found my outer tears again.

As I was going through this extreme bout of facing and working through my depression and bulimia, my Mom sent me cards with inspirational quotes, letting me know that everything was going to be ok.

One morning I received a card from her stating:

Finish each day and be done with it. You have done what you could. Some blunders and absurdities have crept in; forget them as soon as you can. Tomorrow is a new day. You shall begin it serenely and with too high a spirit to be encumbered with your old nonsense. - Emerson

I simply said a little thanks in my head, made a note to say thank you the next time I spoke with her and moved on.

For whatever reason, that was also the day that I had this heaviness weighing on my chest. I just felt lonely and sad, but not sure why. It was just a down day for no reason as can happen.

To help move me through this feeling, I took some action. Grabbing my laptop, I wandered down the street to my favourite coffee cafe where I eagerly started writing to get these lonely feelings out of my head. By doing this, I would get them out of my head, onto "paper" and then not have to think about them anymore. I could simply be done with them – just as the quote on the card suggested.

As the universe would have it, I was writing about how I felt invisible, sad, reflecting on negative past relationships and friendships and blah, blah, blah. After I finished, I closed my laptop, pushing it to the side and pulled out a book to read. Barely a minute passed when the fella at the table next to me picked up his dirty dishes and placed them on the corner of my table, inches away from my laptop. I was in utter shock! Thinking – you couldn't leave the dishes on your table? Did he not see that I was at the table with my own items on it? I couldn't believe how invisible I was at that moment in time. I decided that maybe it would be best if I packed up my stuff and wandered home.

Once home, I threw on my comfy pants and started watching an episode of Dawson's Creek, where I suddenly just let the tears fall down my face. My tear ducts began to work again...and then some. As I was drowning in this tsunami of tears, the phone rang. It was my Mom. Say what you will, but moms definitely have Mama Bear intuition when their cubs are hurting.

Our conversation went like this:

Mom: Hi honey. It's your Mom!

Me: *snort* Hi Mom. How are you?

Mom: Oh, you know. I'm fine. How are you feeling?

Me: *snot running down my face, tears percolating on my eyelids* I'm okay, juu..juus...just having a down day. I got your card though. Thank you.

Mom: You're welcome. Why such a down day?

I proceed to tell her about the coffee shop incident and how I knew that I was being overly emotional and that of course, I'll get back on track and stop feeling this way. I always do. All through this she just kept saying, "Yep. I know you will. Of course I understand. Well, duh!" and "remember what the card says that you just have to forget the absurdities. You know that there are ignorant people out there. You'll be fine." Once all was said, my wonderfully supportive mother threw in one last statement:

Now, go wash your face and swipe on some lipstick. You'll feel better by making yourself feel pretty.

I stopped dead and almost burst out laughing. Never, in my entire life, had I heard something from my mom's mouth sound so 1950's other than when she taught me "we must, we must, we must increase our bust. It's better, it's better, it's better for our sweater."

After an amazing laugh due to the random absurdity of the statement, I felt 1000 times better. I knew that it was just a day of bad timing and in a world where my mom could pull out lines about how lipstick will make me feel better, that I would, of course, be okay.

The next day was a day of smiles…no lipstick needed.

My Own European Beauty

Growing up, I always had issues with my body. Having my first growth spurt while still in my mother's womb, I was always twice the height of the other kids in my classes. Coming from a family that has a tendency for early puberty, I also developed my feminine bits quite a bit earlier than other girls. While I should have been wearing training bras in Grade 3, I tried to not wear them until Grade 5. In hindsight, not such a good idea and probably a cause of my many body woes.

Being raised in a media saturated and body conscious society, I was certainly not the spitting image of what was, and still is, considered the norm. I was not the slender, petite blond that seems to be the preferable body type today. I was quite tall for my age, which also made me heavier than other kids. I would not say that I was fat, but definitely sturdy. Because of this, I mastered the art of changing a shirt over top of another and never showing any skin in the gym change rooms. In the swimming pool change rooms, the only part of my body ever seen was my legs and arms; absolutely nothing of the torso was shown from behind the towel. For all anyone knew, my torso was actually air. And such went my teenage years.

When I was 17, my Mom bought me a day at the spa as a Christmas gift. This gift included a full body massage. Since it was a gift, I could not turn it down. However, I did not enjoy it in the slightest and I certainly did not feel relaxed by the end. The pedicure and manicure were fine. The facial, a little uncomfortable as someone was prodding at my so-called facial flaws, but still bearable. The massage was mortifying!

Lying on a table, with only my jockeys on and a stranger rubbing my nearly naked body remains one of the most traumatizing experiences of my teenage years. No matter how badly I needed a massage after that, and I did need them as a tense and wound-up individual, I refused to go.

All this changed after university when my friend, Jaime, and I travelled Europe. Our first body beauty encounter was on the beach at Cannes. When we first arrived on the beach, everyone around us was wearing next to nothing, sporting incredibly tanned skin. Cautiously, we removed our shorts and shirts (bikinis underneath), revealing our bellies in all their Canadian, pasty white glory. We promptly started to lather up our luscious tummies with SPF 30 sunscreen so we wouldn't burn the part of our bodies that had never seen the light of day. While doing this we noticed that people were looking...no, actually pointing and giggling at how pale and possibly albino like we were in comparison to everyone else around us, making us feel extremely self-conscious. But then something miraculous happened. It seems that our luminous bellies acted like a homing device for the French men. Before we could say "Bonjour!" to the first gentleman, French suitors started coming from every direction to say "hello" and chat with this ghostly creatures. This definitely helped us conquer the bikini body issue we thought we were going to have as we figured that instead of being two reflective Canadians, we were merely two radiating beauties, using the visual version of our pheromones to call in the foreign men. One could say that they were simply blinded by our beauty!

After that day, Jaime and I started to walk with a little extra skip in our step as we made our way through Europe. However, when we went to Turkey, we were not prepared for how comfortable we were about to become with our own body beauty. Jaime and I decided that we needed to truly experience Turkey in all its splendour, so the logical thing to do was have a traditional Turkish bath. We undressed, including our skivvies, in the change room with our towels strategically covering our personal bits. All wrapped up in our towels, we then made our way to the steam room. As we tiptoed into the room we were taken aback by what we saw.

In the middle of the room, there was a huge slab of marble with naked ladies lying on one side of it. On the other side, these large Turkish women were scrubbing daring individuals from head to toe. It took us a couple of seconds before we could comprehend we were going to have to lie in the buff on the marble slab with twenty other naked women. As we slowly walked over to the marble we took extremely deep breaths so we wouldn't pass out (from the heat, of course...not from embarrassment). Looking each other in the eye, we counted to three, threw our towels on the marble slab with our bodies, face down, quickly following. The longer we lay there the more comfortable we became. We noticed that everyone in the bath by no means had the body that we so often saw in Canadian and American media. All the women there were these beautiful, curvy, full-figured ladies, each more comfortable in their skin than the next.

When it was my turn for the Turkish scrub, I began having horrible flash backs to my massage when I was 17, but this time I was completely in the buff and in a room full of other ladies. I hesitantly stood up, grabbed my towel and walked to the other side of the slab. The moment I lay down, on my tummy, the lady started scrubbing; a great exfoliation process I later realized as my bum zit had disappeared when I redressed (we've all had them – tell the truth). It wasn't until the lady slapped me on my bum to communicate that I had to turn over so she could scrub my front that I realized things weren't so bad. I almost burst out laughing at the fact that the only way for her to get my attention was a good ol' slap on my very white rear!

I began to relax as I was able to recognize that this experience was probably one of the most liberating, not humiliating, experiences of my European trip. I, the shy body gal from

Alberta, Canada, was able to lie naked on a marble slab with twenty other women and have a Turkish lady exfoliate me!

When you are able to have your body scrubbed from head to toe in front of a room full of women, you quickly begin to feel comfortable and confident in your own skin. Really, this entire Europe trip was a complete chance for freedom - freedom from negative thoughts, from clothes, and from believing that a white belly isn't sexy.

And now, well I have absolutely no problem going for a massage in a private room!

Accidental Punching Bag

Thankfully I have lasted 30+ years without ever having taken a punch. Even when younger, my older sister and I would only get into fighting matches consisting of the odd slap, a little hair pulling, and a random kick here or there. Usually, while wearing socks on linoleum floors, we would simply put our hands on each other's shoulders and lean on each other until the other would move. When one wanted to be tricky, the other would simply remove their hands, leaving the other to quickly catch themselves before they fell. More often than not...I was the faller.

However, my non-punched self changed when I decided to go bra hunting at Victoria's Secret. After wandering the store, feeling overwhelmed by the number of under options and the amount of padding in the store, I finally found some choices to try on and made my way to the pink change rooms.

As I was trying on one of the bras, I realized that I needed to adjust the straps since, even though it was a push up bra, having my ladies smushed against chin seemed a little too excessive.

I was having difficulty adjusting the right side strap, deciding that it must have been secured with manufacturing strength staples. I quickly realized that the only way to loosen this strap was to use some full force, She-Ra strength. As I was making some leeway, the strap suddenly snapped down, hitting my chest and leaving my already in motion fist to fly with an immense power into the right side of my jaw. Big physics lesson was applied at that moment...right on my face.

As my jaw went numb, stars circling my head, while tears filled my eyes, I prayed that I wouldn't pass out in the change room from the sheer superhuman strength that my jaw just received. I sat down on the bench in the room, contemplating pushing the help button to see if the change room helper could get me some ice to relieve some of the pain. I decided against this for fear that any inkling of pride I carried with me that day would be completely lost if a well put-together sales lady came in and saw me, lopsided boobs – the left one was still up at my chin – frazzled hair, and shame in my eyes.

After a couple minutes, there was a knock on the door and a soft voice called out, "how's everything going in there?" It was then that I realized I would have to leave the change room, hoping that a bruise hadn't begun to appear, while explaining, "oh that? That's from when I sucker punched myself while learning the intricacies of bra straps." Rather, I composed myself and calmly answered, "everything's fine! Just going through my options." As I slowly stood up, finessed myself out of the Super Bra, changed into my "bra for beginners" and put on my top, I decided that maybe push ups weren't really for me.

Despite the pain radiating through my face, in a way I felt a little bit of pride growing inside me that day. Having never been hit in the jaw – or anywhere for that matter – before, I didn't know what to expect. Now, since I unexpectedly punched myself at ultimate fighter force and survived, I know that I can handle a solid punch without causing any major damage to my face.*

*Please note that I am in no way encouraging anyone to try and punch themselves to see if their face can "take it." Just be gentle and kind!

Bahamian Chivalry

In 2011, I decided that it was time for a real vacation, having not been on one in nearly a decade.

I decided to go by myself and have adventures in the just foreign enough, but not so foreign that I would be intimidated, world of the Bahamas!

Travelling by myself for the first time ever, I decided to stay at an all-inclusive resort. Fortunately for me, the staff members at the resort were amazing. In fact, as a single traveller, one of the waiters there, Joe, offered to take me on a day trip on his day off and give me a tour of Nassau. As he put it, his tour would be "a way more in depth tour than the bus tours would provide."

While there was a chance I might not have returned to the resort, my gut said "go" and just enjoy your time. I decided to live a little and, despite what my mom told me when I was little, trust a stranger in the hopes of creating some kind of adventure.

Joe picked me up at 9 am the next day and we set off. At each place we stopped, Joe was the utmost gentleman. He would open doors for me, pay my way into the sites, always let me go in first and wait for me while I did my touristy photo shots. When walking, whenever we came to a curb or some uneven ground, he would always grab my elbow to steady me and make sure I was okay walking. While he may have been doing this simply because I often appear unsteady on my feet, you could tell this was just part of his nature in the presence of, well, a lady.

Having not ever experienced this level of chivalry before from my former Canadian suitors, I would jump sometimes when he placed his hand on my elbow or have a look of confusion when he would open the door for me, and this included the car door. After the fifth time of my jumping at the elbow touch, he finally commented on my reactions.

Joe: You're not used to having a man help you, are you?

Me: Not really. Doesn't happen too often back home.

Joe: Don't the guys there know how to be chivalrous?

Me: Pretty sure they do...it's just not that common.

Joe: Why not? I find that girls are way nicer when you are!

I had to laugh. It was such a simple truth. Filled with ulterior motives, yes, but true none the less.

To this day, when a fella does a chivalrous act of sorts, I always smile, thinking of the hidden truth that they know:

Girls are simply nicer when boys are chivalrous!

Lasik Surgery A-Ok!

Years ago, I scheduled myself for laser eye surgery. I was so excited since I played a lot of sports that had balls and Frisbees flying at my head and swam 3 times a week, yet I could never wear contacts and my glasses just got in the way. I couldn't wait to be active without having to worry about my glasses being broken, or not being able to see when swimming. I was about to regain the 20/20 vision of my youth.

On the night before my surgery, I was utterly exhausted and fell asleep as soon as my head hit the pillow. During the night, I somehow flipped over onto my stomach and tucked both my arms under my chest. Having fallen asleep fairly early, I woke up in the middle of the night and, in my very groggy state, realized that the weight of my body had made my right arm go completely numb. I rolled myself over onto my back, but had to use my left arm to pull my limp right arm from under my body.

In doing this, I, for some odd reason propped my right arm up on its elbow, resting it on my hip, with the hand closed in a delicate fist. However, in my brain, I thought I had lain my arm down beside me. Naturally, I let go of my right arm.

Gravity then took over...

As soon as I let go of my right arm, the arm, along with my fist – however delicate – came falling down towards my face. With my fist, I ended up punching myself in the right eye, jerking my brain into instant alert mode.

After the initial "owww," the first thought that ran through my head was that I might have given myself a black eye and I would then have to reschedule my surgery since I didn't know if black eyes could be lasered!

Luckily this wasn't the case and the surgery went ahead the next day without much hassle (thanks in large part to the Valium the facility kindly hands out to patients).

However, I always wonder that if I had to reschedule, how would I explain punching myself in my own eye and not be the butt end of the company's jokes, or worse, part of their "Do Not Do This" before surgery list, for years to come?

Physical Lessons: Bodies are Great

- Compliments can come from the most random of places. The key is believing them when they come your way.
- Moms usually mean well, even if the advice is a wee out of date. It's the thought behind some advice that is what should be heard.
- Your body is yours and it's like no one else's. Embrace it because someone thinks your body is perfect and wishes they had it.
- Chivalry is not dead. It's just in the Bahamas.
- "Dignity" is but a state of mind. Hold your head high as everyone has their own demons to fight and you have nothing to apologize for.

Public Places

Being in public is really the only place that we can truly come to terms with our quirks. After all, if someone doesn't witness your awkward self, then are you truly awkward?

I Hate Running / Healthy People

A few summers ago, my friend, Julie, wanted to learn how to run and asked if I wanted to join her. Having once been able to run a half marathon, I was definitely out of shape and wanted to get back into tiptop form, so I "enthusiastically" said, "you bet!"

On one of our first runs on the glorious Calgary pathway system, Julie got a cramp in her leg, so we stopped to stretch. As we were stretching beside the pathway, an older gentleman, holding a Frisbee, stopped within an arm's reach of us and simply stared. Not a word was uttered, he just watched. As Julie and I exchanged our "it's time we move" looks, the man nodded his head and walked away. A sort of, "good stretch, ladies. Good, good stretch" nod. Awkward, I remembered why running along the Calgary pathways, while beautiful, had some downfalls.

A couple days later we decided that it was time to try running again, but took a different path. As we were running, we came across two guys and a girl, smoking a cigarette while sitting on a bench. As we were passing them, the girl stood up and shouted at us "I really hate healthy people! Hahahaha!" Julie and I quickly transformed our "slow and steady" pace into our version of a "Usain Bolt" pace. Not just wanting to distance ourselves from the smell of smoke, but from fear of not knowing how deep the gal's hatred for healthy people ran (hee hee – puns), hoping that her lungs wouldn't be able to match the capacity that ours did.

Once far enough, we burst into nervous hysterics, which required us to stop running from laughing so hard…or simply because we were out of breath from our unexpected sprint interval.

We ran a little further and turned around. On our way back we had to pass the trio again. This time we knew better and made sure to put our sprint interval into play as we passed them before any comments could be shouted at us. The minute we were out of their site, without comment or look to one another, we both stopped running suddenly. It was like our bodies told us that we had been healthy enough for the day. While we tried to run again, we just couldn't. Turns out, we realized that while we tried to be healthy, part of our bodies truly hated it too. Something that girl said to us must have reached into the depths of our subconscious and told us "enough...you can be healthy another day. It's time to stop." Each time we started to run again on our journey back home, we felt like we were in cement and would burst out laughing, realizing that sometimes laughter can be the best health boost there is.

A Little Lopsided Luck

Heritage Park in Calgary is a great attraction that shows what the city used to look like well before plumbing was introduced. It was a place I always wanted to go, but never did, even after living here for over five years. One day, a friend of mine simply said, "let's go," so I could finally see what the hubbub was about.

While we were wandering through the old timey streets, Cathy told me all about the times she went there as a little girl when we wandered upon the blacksmith's workshop. She told me that when she was younger, there was a blacksmith who would make little good luck horseshoes for the kid visitors. My friend decided that perhaps what I needed that day was a bit of good luck and asked the lady blacksmith if she could make one for me.

Not overly enthused, the blacksmith reluctantly agreed and began to work away at this small good luck horseshoe. (Cathy was always great at convincing people). After a half hour, much metal pounding, and a few grumbles later, the good luck shoe was complete. It was huge and could easily have been fitted for a stuffed My Little Pony. Not the petite shoe we were expecting, but still a great shoe. The truly funny thing wasn't the size of it, but that the shoe ended up being lopsided!

It made me laugh so hard because, just like this good luck horseshoe, life had a way of having lopsided luck sometimes…but it would always balance itself out.

To this day, I cherish this horseshoe, always bringing it with me wherever I go, just in case I need a wee bit of lopsided luck.

A Banker's Hall Breakdown

Prior to starting my own company, I worked for a professional services business in downtown corporate Calgary and often walked through Banker's Hall on my way home. Banker's Hall is the hub of all that is corporate – men in pinstriped suits, women in heels with not a hair out of place, cell phone conversations galore; there was always hustle and bustle.

One day after working late, I made my way through a virtually empty Banker's Hall when suddenly I just started to uncontrollably cry. I couldn't stop and my breath was becoming short and very staggered. I realized that I was having a full-blown panic attack in the middle of the corporate world. This world is not the place you want to have a breakdown.

Fortunately I was able to find a bench to sit down and start texting with a friend who calmed me down with her kindness.

However, while I was having this attack, there were a few things that suddenly became so clear to me. Banker's Hall's layout is open in the middle from top to bottom, allowing sunlight from the roof windows to shine throughout the building. As I was sitting on the second floor of the building I looked up and noticed that on the third floor were four security guards staring down at crying me. Two had smirks on their faces, the other two looked with widened eyes, shocked at seeing this uncontrollably sobbing girl on a bench. I thought to myself...out loud...either go do your job or come and see if you can help me, just quit staring!

By this point, my breathing had become much more regular thanks to my friend; the tears weren't streaming from my eyes any longer and the flow of the nose had slowed down to a slight dribble. Still feeling a mess, I decided to make my way home.

Once in the comfort of my stretchy pants and wrapped in my favourite blanket, I reflected on how the whole circumstance took place, realizing just how ridiculous the situation was. After all, I'm sure that the walls of Banker's Hall have seen more than one breakdown during its time standing and those poor security guards were simply frozen in wonderment.

Looking back, it's easier to recognize that my breaking point before being put on anti-depressants would have been quite the sight for anyone to witness makes me laugh, not because this is typically funny. Rather, it's the ludicrousness in the situation, not the sadness.

This incident is the first time I was able to look at depression as humorous, not because I was having a breakdown, but because of the absurdity of circumstances. Even in the darkest moments, there is always a bit of humour, even if it's four large security guards being rendered motionless by a then frail and teary-eyed girl.

Hearing Aids the Heart

Shoppers Drug Mart has always been my favourite place to stock up on toiletries. Most times, I can get in and out in a matter of minutes as I know my mission and the checkouts move swiftly. Then there was the time that the entire store was in the checkout line at the same time, while the "register in training" was on till. Time was standing still. Usually a huge irritant for me, this time around I was able to remain calm as I put the "counting to 10" technique into practice.

As I was waiting, the lady behind me shouted, "Mom! Mom! We're over here, in the line up." Startled from my counting, I was very curious as to who "Mom" was. Casually looking over my shoulder I saw an older woman in her 80s looking at the magazines, showing no signs of having heard anything. The lady behind me then mumbled under her breath, "I cannot wait until we get her a hearing aid."

I tried to hold it in, but I just couldn't, and with that, I let out a laugh snort that shook my shoulders. I turned around and, in the Canadian way, said "sorry," since it was obvious that I had been eavesdropping. Luckily the lady started to laugh herself saying, "I should really remember that no one else around me needs a hearing aid." We had a good chuckle with one another as she told me how she almost convinced her mom to get a hearing aid the week before until one of her mom's friends started going on about how much of a nuisance they were. "Curses," the lady said as she jokingly shook her fist in the air.

It was then my turn at the till where I paid and started on my journey home. As I walked home, I had to smile remembering past phone conversations with my Grandmother. Every call we had in the last few years of her life started with her testing the controls to get the volume of her hearing aid just right, often requesting that I say, "hello! Hello! HELLO!" into the phone numerous times until she found a setting that was perfect. It often felt like we were testing a microphone and, while it was definitely an annoyance to her, it certainly almost always made us smile when we finally chatted.

I'm sure her hearing aid was a nuisance indeed, but it never ceased to bring a giggle to both of us.

Guilty Pleasure Let Go

It's time for some real honesty:

1. I love going to coffee shops and not just because I have an obsession with, well, coffee. I find that a coffee shop is the perfect place to have session after session of people watching experiences, imagining each individual's unique story.

2. I also love the *Twilight* books. They are my guilty pleasure reading material and often calm my brain when there are too many thoughts overwhelming my head. However, I never read these books in public because they're too heavy to lug around and, while I know it shouldn't, my love of these books embarrasses me. Clearly I am not a tween, the key audience for this series, but a 30-something year old woman for goodness sake!

When the final Twilight movie, *Breaking Dawn: Part 2*, was released to theatres, I decided that it was time for me to reread the series to get all refreshed with the details of the stories. Starting with the first book, I was reading away at home when I just had the urge to go to out to a coffee shop for some extra caffeine and coffee shop buzz.

I hummed and hawed about taking the book or my laptop with me, ultimately deciding on the book. I figured what were the chances that the one day I decide to bring my guilty pleasure out into public with me, that I would find myself having to explain this pleasure.

I made it to my fave coffee shop and settled into a comfy booth with my coffee, puff wheat square, and book. I was engrossed in my reading, cozy in my booth, and simply enjoying the smells (coffee) and sounds (whirring machines, people chatting, plates clinking, music) of the cafe. At that moment, this tall cutie, a regular at the shop, sauntered up to me and asked what I was reading.

I could tell that he was expecting something much more thought provoking, so was a little taken aback by me hesitancy in telling him. Sheepishly I looked up and slowly flipped my book to show the cover. He could tell by my face – bright red cheeks, down cast eyes, and deep "don't judge me" breath – that it was one of those guilty pleasures that we all have for no rhyme or reason and I didn't really want to talk about it.

He quickly said, "Don't worry. I know I shouldn't, but I love *My Name is Earl*. I completely understand loving something that you don't want to, but just can't help."

It was then that I realized I needed to embrace my love of *Twilight*. Everyone has their very own Twilight-type guilty pleasure, so there's no need for being embarrassed. And with that, I finished my coffee (and the chapter I was on) and walked home, proudly carrying my book, title showing and all, with my head held high.

All this being said, I'm pretty sure that I won't be taking my *Twilight* books with me to the coffee shop again (unless I finally invest in a Kindle, of course).

Internet Dating Fiasco

I, like many a single woman in Calgary and prior to meeting Andy, tried Internet dating on numerous occasions. While I didn't found my ultimate love online, I definitely gained many an entertaining story. Stories that leave me with the "what was that?" feeling at the end of the "date."

While there had been many a first date for me online, there were two in particular that really stood out, probably because they were slightly more creepy than entertaining.

Denny's Boy

When we first started emailing, Denny's Boy and I seemed to have a lot in common. So much so that we finally decided to meet in person and chat over a cup of coffee.

While I was thinking the typical Starbucks or Second Cup, he suggested Denny's. I was a little shocked when he suggested this, and said yes without thinking. Besides, it would be an interesting place for a first date, right? Date scheduled - Monday at 7 pm at Denny's.

I showed up at 6:59 pm and he was already there, a full coffee cup already in the middle of the table.

It was awkward conversation from the get go...possibly because he hadn't used his real picture, or at least a recent one to say the least, and I was trying to figure out why someone would do that.

I mean, don't get me wrong, there were slight similarities – his height and hair colour – but other than that, he did not look at all the same.

RED FLAG 1!!!

As we continued the conversation, he asked me if I had used any other sites than the dating site we "met" on. To which I responded, "Yep" and named the other site. Denny's Boy asked me how many matches on the other site I was connected with and I told him a couple hundred. He mentioned that he tried to use that same site, but after he filled out their initial questionnaire, he received a notice saying that his answers didn't warrant any matches and he should look elsewhere for his love match. Curious, it was a multiple choice questionnaire, so surely he would have been matched with somebody. I wondered just how, exactly, did he answer the questions about hobbies, family, values, and so on, that he didn't have a single match.

RED FLAG 2!!!

We then continued our talk when it occurred to me that he hadn't had a single sip from the coffee cup. In fact, he was actually drinking lemonade. So, I decided to draw attention to this fact, the coffee elephant if you will.

Me: Not really feeling like having your coffee, I see.

DB: Oh, I don't like coffee

Me: Ooookay. Then why did you order it?

DB: Well, I figured this is what chatting over a cup of coffee meant.

RED FLAG 3!!!

While this move could have been pretty cute, there just seemed to be a few too many red flags at this point and it turned it into an odd, get out of there moment, rather than something to laugh at.

Thankfully, the conversation was pretty much stunted after that and the evening was done. I've never really been able to chat over a cup of coffee the same way again. Drink it, you bet. Chat…not so much.

After the date ended, I reflected on the big online dating lesson I learned: tone and personality over email can be misinterpreted. What might be read as sarcastic and funny in your head is actually creepy and completely serious in person. Hence, meeting in a public place is always the way to go.

Husky Guy

I met Husky Guy on the same site as Denny's Boy. Like DB, the email conversation went well and we decided to have a quick in-person conversation on a Thursday evening.

This time, we agreed to meet at Starbucks (I learned my lesson about Denny's). The beginning of the date was going fairly well. Conversation flowed easily enough, he was quite cute, and it seemed like we had a lot in common, until he asked me what I took in university. I told him that I had my Bachelor of Arts and majored in Sociology. What followed left me completely speechless, with no way of reacting without drawing attention from the other tables around us.

HG: I took a sociology class once, but I didn't do very well in it.

Me: Oh. Why not?

HG: My professor didn't really like my final paper.

Me: What did you write it on?

HG: I compared the liberation of women to liberating my family's Husky Dog.

Me: *blink followed by stunned silence*

HG: I basically said that we had liberated my Husky too fast and it ended up getting hit by a car because she hadn't learned to not run out onto the road. I then said that the women's liberation movement happened too fast and that women weren't prepared to have the equal opportunities that they were then given.

Me: *blink followed by stunned silence*

HG: I think my professor was a feminist.

RED FLAGS GALORE!!!!!!!!!!!!!!!!!

Me: Umm...you do know that women's liberation wasn't very quick and you're comparing women to your dog, right? I'm going to say that I'm on the side of your professor here.

The conversation pretty much went south after that as I didn't have the patience to deal with someone who believed that women and dogs are interchangeable. After that, I drove home in a bit of fog. While funny that there was someone who could believe this, I – probably quite naively – was flabbergasted that this belief was out there.

Needless to say, with so many red flags on the last two fellows, I pretty much gave up with Internet dating after that, choosing to focus primarily on my own self development.

Glove or G-love?

One day my friend, Valerie, and I were driving down Macleod Trail and this bright, flashing sign caught my eye. First thing to note is that this is really not the safest thing to have going on a busy road, but...that's Calgary! Fortunately, I was in the passenger's seat.

The letters G L O V E flashed across and after I spelled it all out, I asked my friend, "G Love...what's that?"

Valerie, with a "you can't be serious" tone, "Ummm..."

It suddenly clicked for me - "GLOVE!!! Ohhhhhh...not G Love. That makes no sense at all!" And then I realized the sign was on the side of a motorcycle clothing store.

Yep, glove makes way more sense than G Love.

BUT...the question still remains, is there such a thing as G Love?

Snakes - My Ultimate Fear

When Andy and I first started dating, we decided to go on a daytrip to Drumheller to see the dinosaurs at the Royal Tyrrell Museum. Not having been there since I was eight, I loved every second of wondering around, looking at all the different ages and dino bones.

However, since wandering around the museum only took us 3 hours, Andy asked if we could go to Reptile World too, just to make an entire day of it. After all, it was only 2:00 pm and Drumheller's only 90 minutes from Calgary, so the drive home would be very short.

The first thing to realize here is that Reptile World is full of snakes. The one thing that sends shivers down my spine, while simultaneously leaving me a sweaty mess of fear. Ever since I was little, I've had this irrational fear of snakes, so much so that I still dream that they are under the covers of my bed. In fact, when I was seven, I was convinced that there were snakes under my sheets, so I refused to actually sleep under my covers. Rather, I chose to sleep on top of the bedspread, covered with a simple afghan that I could quickly escape from should the snakes try to crawl in. Despite this fear of snakes, I nervously answered, "yes," to Reptile World. Besides, they also had all kinds of colourful frogs, so how could the place be all bad?

Upon arriving at Reptile World we were pleasantly greeted by a huge tortoise wandering around the building. He was super friendly and even let me take a couple pictures of him. Well, he may not have been super friendly, just slow.

I was gradually getting comfortable in the building, releasing the tension in my hands as I tried to be rational, telling my self that all the snakes were all behind glass and couldn't get to me.

Just as my shoulders were finally lowering down from my ears, we rounded a corner where one of the snake handlers was holding a huge boa constrictor named Brittany (seriously, who names a SNAKE Brittany?). Andy, excited by seeing the boa outside its cage, quickly walked up to the handler and started petting Brittany. While I stood beside Andy, I could feel my hands starting to clench up, my shoulders jumping up to my earlobes again, and eyes forgetting to blink. Worried that this currently docile creature would lash out at any second and bite me, I envisioned all kinds of poisonous venom coursing through my entire body, leaving me to die in a crumpled mess on the floor.

Thankfully, that didn't happen and Andy didn't make me touch Brittany. I was past the point of trying to impress Andy by being a daredevil and focused more on being endearing through my fears. We continued on our journey as I practiced calming breaths.

Still shaken by our encounter with the boa, we were looking at one of the crocodiles when two girls, around four or five in age, walked in front of us smiling, holding something in their hands. I smiled back and said, "What do you have there?" Then, my eyes bulged out of my head and I screamed, "Oh my god! It's a snake." Quickly running away from them, I turned back to see their mom and Andy laughing at me since both girls had small, *rubber* toy snakes that they were carrying around.

With my pride and dignity removed, I walked back to Andy, head hanging low.

As we walked away from the bewildered children, I frantically said to Andy, "It's possible the handler would let kids walk around with tinier snakes...it really is!"

Andy simply gave my arm a little "there, there" pat while trying to get his laughter under control. We left soon after that, Andy still giggling behind my back.

All in all, I am definitely proud of myself for even agreeing to go to Reptile World and facing my fear of snakes. Well, not facing per se since I ran away, but still staying in the same vicinity as these devil creatures.

Princess Faints-A-Lot

The very first time I fainted I was 14. I don't remember fainting, I just remember being shaken awake and then given a glass of water. The next time, I was 20 in a university sociology class, watching a fairly disturbing movie about the effects of heroin and the next thing I remember was my friend shaking me awake and sharing his water bottle with me. In both situations, while I can chuckle at them, I definitely had a bit of ego stripped away.

After the incident in class, I stopped fainting for years. That is until I had the swine flu of 2009. I had been home for a couple of days from work and had run out of juice and soup, the two staples that I was living off of. While I was not even close to feeling better, against my better judgment, I decided to drive over to Safeway to pick up some supplies for the next few days.

Being a single, independent gal at the time (still independent!), it never occurred to me to call anyone to pick up these items and drop them off for me, especially since it was the middle of a weekday and everyone was at work.

To leave, I decided that putting on somewhat appropriate outdoor clothes would be best. I slowly put on my "classy" stretchy comfy pants, hoodie, and big purple knit toque since 1) I hadn't showered in a couple days, and 2) I didn't really care about being all pretty while walking through Safeway. I just wanted to get in, grab my soup and juice, pay, and get back home to bed.

The cold air from my car to the Safeway entrance was actually refreshing, convincing me that I was totally going to make this trip a success. However, as I walked around Safeway, I started to feel overheated and lightheaded. I wondered if I should give up my quest for juice and just leave, but determined, I forced myself to finish and get to the checkout as quickly as possible. There had to be a result of this journey and arriving home with juice was my personal Everest to conquer.

As the cashier, a much smaller gal than my European roots self rang my items through, the heat started to become unbearable and I started seeing black spots. When she told me the total, my knees started to buckle and I felt myself falling. The cashier quickly took action and ran around to catch me as I was going down. Being the 5'9" woman that I am, it must have been a sight to see as this tiny 5'2", slim built girl try to pick me up. She ended up calling over her boss and they half dragged, half walked me to the Safeway Starbucks, got me some ice cold water, and let me get my bearings as to what had just happened.

Being quite shaken, and embarrassed, I didn't really feel like I should be driving my car home. Walking was also out of the question as it would have been a 25-minute walk. I had no idea what to do, so I called my work, which was a 5-minute drive away. Luckily, my boss, Brent, was so kind, he came and picked me up to drive me home.

The first thing Brent said to me when he came in to get me was, "That's a stupid looking toque." I didn't have the energy to fight back that it was actually really cute and he just didn't have any fashion sense (I still wear it to this day). He then asked if I had actually bought my juice and soup yet, to which I shamefully responded, "No." Brent quickly picked these items up, bought them and then drove me home, where I got a wee lecture on why I should always call someone for help me if need be. No more of this incredible, "I can do it all" mentality. I simply said, "thank you, you're right," and made my way back inside my home.

After my pride recovered a bit, I was able to see the extreme humour in this scenario of the 5'9" lady fainting on a 5'2" slender gal, and having to be saved by her boss. The next week when I was well enough to go back to work, I was certainly in for a humbling experience as Brent had told everyone what had happened. In fact, sitting on my desk, was a juice box. I still don't know who left it there, but it makes me smile.

I have certainly learned my lesson and now call people when I'm too sick to go out. After all, I may not always have someone with ant-like strength to catch me mid-air when fainting!

Other than some bruising of my pride, the truly sad thing about this situation is that I had brought my reusable shopping bag with me and left it at the till after I fainted...causing me to lose this bag. To this day, I have to comfort myself by the fact that it was only $0.99.

Always Remember To Say Please and Thank You

I have often been told that I say please and thank more often than needed. It's not something I do consciously and certainly not something I've always done. However, when I was four, I learned a tough lesson about manners that forever changed the course of my life.

This lesson happened during my second year of preschool, a time of learning how to properly write a capital "E." One day, there was a girl who had a birthday and, as a treat for the entire class, she handed out small packets of crayons to everyone. They were the glorious four pack crayons of red, yellow, blue and green, heaven to a pre-schooler.

All the students had to sit around in a circle and wait while the birthday girl and one of the teachers handed them out. When she got to me, she gave me the packet and I simply took it...no thank you at all as I didn't realize it was needed. Looking back, I should have since EVERY OTHER KID in the circle did.

The teacher stopped and said to me, "Now Lindsay, what do you say?" Being four, I wasn't too sure what she was asking and simply shrugged my shoulders in an "I dunno" fashion.

With the rest of the class looking on, I was so embarrassed that she had stopped and drew this kind of attention to me. I could feel the red in my cheeks rising, spreading all the way up to my ears. Even from a young age I knew that I absolutely hated having any kind of attention on me, particularly of the negative kind. I much more preferred being in the background.

After I shrugged, the teacher forcefully took the crayons from my tiny hands, and said, "You have to say 'thank you' for the gift you are being given. Can you say 'thank you'?"

I could feel my inner stubborn side bubbling up and coupling with my embarrassment. With this combination of feelings, I wasn't going to budge at this point, so I looked down at the floor and simply said, "No." Ego was never very pretty on me.

The teacher, none too pleased, told me "Then you will not get the crayons. Good girls and boys say 'please' and 'thank you.' Do you understand?"

With my eyes still focused on the floor, I simply nodded. She then went on to say, "If you feel like you can say 'thank you' we can try this again."

I sat there while the rest of the crayons were handed out. For the rest of the day I was pretty quiet as I tried to get over my embarrassment, thinking that I was being judged and laughed at by all the other four year olds.

Never wanting to feel that way again about something so simple, I ALWAYS say please, thank you, sorry, and many other forms of appreciation so that I never have to relive the embarrassment I felt that day. This is a lesson that has served me well since that day.

The other lesson I took away?

Crayons really aren't that great anyways.

The True Definition of NERVOUS

Whoever told me that I would never have to parallel park after my driver's test was LYING. If you are reading this and don't have your licence yet, practice your parallel parking. You will absolutely need this skill if you plan of parking at some point.

Being a freelance writer, I am constantly having to drive to a client's office to meet with them. As such, I often end up having to go into downtown Calgary, right smack dab in the middle of the afternoon when parking is sparse and aggressive drivers are abundant.

One such client meeting day, I found myself driving around for 15 minutes (record time) when I finally saw two shining, open spots that one could easily slide into without any hassle. Unfortunately, I was on a one-way street, two lanes over from the spots, with no time to quickly dash over to the glorious openness.

I ended up driving around a couple blocks to get back (as per the many one-way streets downtown). Once back on the block where the spots were, I immediately moved into the proper lane, ready to drive right into MY spot. But, when I got there, an Audi had parked in the first open spot, leaving me to have to parallel in the second. As I lined myself up with the Audi to properly pull into my spot, I noticed the Audi driver standing beside her car, watching as I attempted to park. It was then that I realized that the other car I would be parking in front of was a Range Rover. Of course! My first parallel park in years and I had to be parking between 2 expensive, high-end vehicles, one of which had the owner intently watching. EEP!

Having flashbacks to my driver's test where I had to try parallel parking three times before I got it, I quickly felt my Secret deodorant kick in under my arms, while a single bead of sweat drizzled down the side of my face. In that moment I thought, "Well, at least I'll still smell fresh as a daisy for my client."

I took a deep breath, remembered my drivers training, and slowly backed in, then straightened forward, then centred myself in the spot, all in one shot, like a complete pro. I was ecstatic. Shouting "Ahhhhh yeah!" as I put my car in park. I then made eye contact with the Audi driver. She gave me a slight head nod of, "Good job. I knew you could do it," but her eyes spoke of pure relief.

It was then I realized what the true definition of nervousness was:

The feeling of discomfort and unease as one attempts to parallel park a car for the first time in years, between two expensive, high-end vehicles, while the owner of one said vehicle watches with baited breathe. Best combated by extra strength antiperspirant, deep breathing, and lots of prayer.

How to Run a Half-Marathon

While I do run, it is not my favourite thing to do and I will never fully understand why I chose to run a half marathon in October 2010. Something about setting a goal and reaching it I suppose.

As I was not a runner, I knew that I had to some serious training to do. So, in June 2010, I signed up for the Running Room's Half Marathon Clinic. After hundreds of kilometers and friendships forge, I knew I was ready to run the Victoria Half Marathon that was taking place on Thanksgiving Weekend.

I also justified that the Victoria Half was the one for me rather than any local Calgary ones since 1) my parents reside in Victoria (free lodging, yay!) and 2) it was Thanksgiving, so I would have no guilt about have two, three or even four pieces of pie after I finished my half.

The morning of the run, I started having butterflies in my stomach. "How can I do this?" and "There are so many people here - how am I not going to come in last?" and "This is going to be tricky without my running buddy with me." But, the buzzer went and all us runners began to herd ourselves through the starting gate. In fact, I believe there were a few cows mooing, just to show us humans how to properly make our way through a gate.

After about 30 minutes of running, we were finally spread out enough to develop our own pace. It was just at this moment that the route took us on to Johnson Street, a street I was fully aware would be filled with the cutest boutique shops. Just as I thought I might pass out from trying to powerhouse this half, a sweater in a store window caught my eye, helping me to slow down my pace (thank goodness). In the next few minutes I realized my new motivation for finishing this race: if I successfully completed this half marathon, I would come back to the store the next day and buy that sweater! I quickly took account of what store it was, feeling renewed and ready to run the other 15k left of my half.

About 2 hours later (slow and steady mentality...and what this body allows), I crossed the finished line and was promptly met by my parents shouting their congratulations at me.

As we made our way back to the car, I told my mom that we had to come back to Johnson Street the next day so I could buy a sweater that I saw on my run. My mom turned to me, chuckling as she said,

"You really are my daughter. Only a Harle girl could spot a piece of clothing that we wanted while in our most uncomfortable state – running, gasping for air, and feeling every muscle of our body – and remember what store a cute sweater is at."

Needless to say, the next day we went back and I bought the sweater, telling the store owner that I saw it on the window mannequin while I was running my half. Surprised by this, she indicated that the next year she knew how to promote her store during the 2011 half!

Note that I did not go back the next year to see if she put this advertising into place...but I'd like to believe she did.

Public Lessons: Anonymous...Maybe...

- There are two kinds of people in public: those who will ignore you and those who want to talk and help. Both provide insight into who they are, not who you are.
- Online dating is a great place to find interesting...characters.
- People shouldn't read signs while driving.
- Being out in public lets you see a whole different world, whether you are observing or participating. Each world will contain lessons. Some will be deep, like not every person is willing to help you. Others, not so much, like sweaters sell really well when placed on a high foot traffic street (business owners - pay attention). Take the lesson, no matter its size, and grow.
- Always say please and thank you...and know when to put your pride aside.

Food and Other Incidents

Yes, food has been a demon for me throughout my own depression constipation. However, food has also brought some of the fondest memories and biggest laughs I have ever had. Food has the power to bring humour to the entire world.

Christmas Dinner Memories

My parents are originally from Ottawa, Ontario, but ended up settling in Alberta to raise my sister and I. This meant that every few years we would all make the journey to Ottawa for a good ol' family visit. While we didn't live nearby, my parents weren't going to let us grow up not knowing our extended family. Thank goodness, otherwise I would never have become the quirky gal I am today.

For Christmas 1987, we flew out to Ottawa for a holiday visit, a very daring feat for my parents to travel with my eight-year-old sister and my five-year-old self. We left on Boxing Day and stayed with my Dad's parents, my Granny and Grandpa. Travelling, at least to me, went off without a hitch, with all luggage arriving and flights on time, at least according to the time that I could tell at that point.

Our first night in Ottawa, we had dinner at my Granny and Grandpa's. My Granny cooked long and hard to serve ham, scalloped potatoes and green beans. Having never had ham or scalloped potatoes before, I eagerly tucked into this new food only to discover it was disgusting! The texture of the ham was so thick and rubbery and the scalloped potatoes were just too rich for my young little tummy. But, not wanting to upset anyone or hurt my Granny's feelings (after all, the woman could cook and bake like no other), I ate as much as I could without making a peep. Later that evening as my Mom tucked me into bed she let me know she knew I didn't like the dinner, but was very proud of me for not getting upset or saying anything.

I went to bed thinking that this new kind of food was behind me for good and the rest of the trip was going to be so much fun.

Little did I know...

The next evening we all went over to my Mom's parents' (my Grandmother and Grandfather) house for dinner. It was a grand and rather loud event with aunts, uncles and cousins.

When dinner was ready, we all sat down to dinner, with me placed between my Mom and my aunt. As the dinner plates began to be passed around, I noticed that each plate contained, yet again, ham, scalloped potatoes, and green beans. I sat there trying to contain how upset I was, as I knew that I just couldn't handle this dinner again. But, like a trooper, I didn't say anything. After more and more plates went around the table, one was finally set in front of me. As I stared at my plate of ham, scalloped potatoes, and green beans, I felt my eyes well up. Slowly, silent tears started to fall down my pudgy, freckle covered cheeks, but I refused to make a sound.

My mom, noticing these wee tears, leaned down and asked what was wrong.

Me: "Nothing."

Mom: "Are you sure?"

Me: *head nod*

Mom: "Is it the ham and scalloped potatoes?"

Me: *slow head nod*

Mom: "Okay - you don't have to eat it. You did such a good job last night and you're being so good right now. Let's go make you a sandwich and then you can have a nap."

With that, she and my aunt took me to the kitchen and made me the most heavenly PB&J sandwich ever and then put me down for a little nap.

To this day my Mom tells everyone she meets this story...even people I have never met. Nearly thirty years later, when we go over to someone's house for dinner, they always say to me that we are having ham, scalloped potatoes, and green beans with a slight smirk on their face. I will forever be known not as the girl who cries over spilled milk, but as the girl who silently cries over ham, scalloped potatoes, and green beans.

As for me, I have started to take a liking to scalloped potatoes, but the thought of a thick slice of ham still brings back my 5-year-old tears.

Three-Minute Chocolate Cake

When my sister graduated from McGill University in Montreal, my mom and I drove from Edmonton to Montreal to pick her up and move her back home. On the journey back, we made a trip through Niagara-on-the-Lake to take in a few plays at the Shaw Festival.

One night while going out to dinner, we all decided that yes, we should in fact have dessert. Being the healthy beings that we were trying to be on this trip (it didn't really happen), we chose to split one small piece of chocolate cake between the three of us. As we ordered this, we proudly said, "with three forks, please," in an effort to show our waiter how healthy we were being.

Promptly bringing over our cake and three forks, he set the plate in the middle of the table saying, "Enjoy, ladies." He had barely turned his back when we all pounced, eating the cake as if it was the last piece of cake in the world. We tried to savour each bite, but I can honestly say it didn't really happen that way.

We finished in about 3 minutes. The fastest anyone has ever finished something, I'm sure.

The waiter, who had just made his way back to the prep station, saw that we had finished in his short distance. Turning on his heels, he came back to take away our dirty dishes. As he was clearing everything he said, "Wow...you ladies devoured that. I don't think I've ever seen a dessert disappear that quickly."

We all politely chuckled with a slightly embarrassed tinge in our giggle. But, when he walked away my mom leaned in to my sister and I and said, "We're three grown women and that was a tiny piece of cake. He should have kept his mouth shut if he wanted to keep his big tip." I think my Mom would didn't get an even third of the cake...

As true as my Mom's statement was, we all learned a valuable lesson about eating cake when at a restaurant:

1. Take your time when eating dessert. There will always be more cake;
2. Make sure that if you're sharing a dessert that it is going to be a HUGE piece of cake. This way, you can avoid any timing of, and subsequent commentary on, your eating; and
3. When thinking about dessert, it is almost always best to order two instead of one.

Grilled Cheese Meeting

Prior to moving in with Andy, I lived in the best apartment complex, where I started my writing business.

One weekday when I was working away, my stomach started to percolate with hunger growls. I decided to make myself a delicious grilled cheese sandwich as a reward for working oh so hard. Simply put, yum.

With my kitchen right beside my workspace, I put my sandwich in the frying pan to let it start grilling, then went back to my computer to write. I got a wee bit distracted when all of a sudden I smelt burning. Running the 2 feet from my computer to the stove (yep – it was a close-knit apartment...how, oh how, did I not immediately notice the burning?), I quickly turned the heat down on the stove, flipped the sandwich over to the other side and finished cooking. Not to burn both sides of my sandwich, I stood at the stove the entire second half of cooking. I decided that the burnt side really wasn't all that burnt...and boy did I ever enjoy that grilled cheese, even though the smell of burning remained as ventilation in my apartment wasn't all that great.

10 minutes after eating, I had to go out to run a few errands. With my apartment located right in front of the elevators, the burnt smell of my lunch was still wafting through the cracks in the door. While waiting for the elevator, my neighbour, Penny, came out to go down and do her laundry. We got to chatting and she said, "Mmmm....smells like someone's cooking something delicious!" I looked at her and while grimacing I told her, "Ummm...not really...I kind of burnt my grilled cheese sandwich. You're smelling burnt bread and cheese."

"Oh! It doesn't really smell like burnt toast. No one would ever know that you burnt your lunch." She was very kind.

It was at that moment I felt a little relief thinking that perhaps my door has awesome aroma prevention powers that wouldn't allow others to smell what's happening in my apartment. This awesome aroma diffusion ensured that people would never know when I truly messed up the simplest of foods.

And with that, I made many a grilled cheese sandwich every week.

Lessons on Talking with Strangers

This tale did not happen to me, but my friend Julie. When she and her husband, Dwayne, tag-teamed to tell me this story, I laughed so hard, tears rolled down my eyes.

Dwayne and Julie were having a great night out, celebrating their friend Amy's birthday by going to see a play with her and her boyfriend. After the play they met up with some other peeps at a bar and continued celebrating all things Amy.

After an hour, Dwayne and Julie were eager to go as super social situations could be overwhelming, but felt that the time to leave had not quite come yet. It was at this point that they were drawn into a fairly intense conversation with a random stranger. It was one of those run-ins that happen at any good ol' Canadian pub.

Described to me as 'a burly man with one of the biggest beards' that Julie or Dwayne has ever seen, Burly Man spoke with a ferociousness that would have frightened Goliath.

During this conversation, Burly Man was eating a late night snack and had no fear of speaking with his mouth full. It was on one of his intense mouth-filled monologues when the event happened...a piece of his half-chewed food flew out of his mouth and landed in Julie's open mouth as she was trying to respond.

Julie sat there in complete and utter shock taking in what just happened when she realized that she still had the food in her mouth. Desperate not to swallow Burly Man's half chewed food, she sneakily spit it out in a napkin so not to cause a scene or accidentally insult Burly Man's generosity in sharing his snack.

Dwayne and Julie decided that with Burly Man's 'sharing,' it was officially time to go. They quickly said their good-byes and took off in a hurry.

On the drive home, they were chatting about what had happened when Dwayne said, "I didn't want to tell you in there, but you realize that Burly Man is an avid tobacco chewer, so you ended up having not only his chewed up food in your mouth...but tobacco too."

Julie asked Dwayne to pull over as she dry heaved out the side of the car. This reaction, in my opinion, was completely warranted.

While I know that one should be very sympathetic to their friend at this point, which I am, there is just something beyond amusing about imaging this happen. How did those few seconds line up for this one bit of flying food? Did some higher power align this moment for their amusement? Or, was this merely a coincidence?

All I can say is that ever since that day, Julie has been very careful when she is around other people who are eating and talking.

The Truth about Almond Milk

A while back, I switched to using almond milk instead of skim milk. While I tell people that normal milk didn't sit very well with me and almond milk was a healthy alternative, the truth behind it is much more...strategic.

First, you're probably wondering why do I tell people this. Well, the type of milk one uses somehow comes up in conversations quite a bit. Next, why am I lying about my milk switching? Well, it all has to do with Kraft Dinner.

You see, I just LOVE Kraft Dinner (better known to us Canadians as KD). Growing up, this delicious neon orange pasta was served in my house as a special treat. When I saw the fluorescent orange elbow pasta staring up at me, I did a happy giggle dance, thrilled that this was the dinner I was about to eat.

When I permanently moved out on my own, KD became a dinner staple. Quickly turning into a couple weekly meals, rather than the every few months I grew up with, I eventually found myself no longer completing my happy giggle dance when I took the first glowing bite. After much humming and hawing, I made the dreadful decision that I should no longer have KD until I could get as excited about it as I once did as a child. The only problem – HOW do I stop buying it? Will power would simply not be enough.

My solution! Take away the proper ingredients you need to make it, namely the milk.

I had heard about almond milk, but never thought to try it. I bought my first litre, just to test it out, and quickly learned that no, it really did not make good KD. I thought, "Brilliant! This is the perfect way to ensure that I do not buy any KD since I won't have the proper milk to make it delicious! And really, what's the point if it's not any good?"

Ever since then I have been using almond milk not as a healthy alternative for cow's milk...but as my healthy alternative for countering my Kraft Dinner addiction.

And now, when KD is placed in front of me, my happy giggle dance begins in my hips...

Candy Corn Conundrum

My love for candy corn is sometimes detrimental to my health and not just because of the obvious processed sugar overloading reason.

I have readily admitted that I can be a bit of a klutz from time to time, but I believe that candy corn enhances this quality 10 fold in me. Fortunately, I am able to steer clear of this deliciousness for 11 months of the year. It's really only in October, when Shoppers Drug Mart sells buckets of candy corn, that I am tempted by, and often succumb to, my yellow/white/orange cravings.

One Halloween in particular, after a very successful candy corn munching session, I put the lid back on my bucket, while contemplating what the calorie count of my latest corn devotion was.

As I was walking back to my pantry, I decided I needed to know. Worried that if I turned the bucket upside down, all my candy corn would fall out, I choose to lift the bucket up over my head, turning my neck at an awkward angle to look under the bucket at nutritional info sticker. At this moment I bashed the top of my head into the corner of my wall. After the initial shock, I shook off the pain, and started to laugh. Once I took a breath, I had the epiphany that I probably could have simply flipped the bucket over since there was a lid on it; no candy corn would have spilt out.

Having been privileged to many of my "walk into walls" moments, I immediately texted my friend Cindy. Her response was simple: "Bwahahahaha. Typical."

It was at this moment based on Cindy's lack of shock on my wall crash, that I realized my candy corn addiction created many a conundrum for my physical safety, namely a significant decrease in my usually logical brain due to sugar overdosing.

In the meantime, while I work through my addiction, I decided that I would be well served to investigate ways to aesthetically bubble wrap the walls of my home just in case I wouldn't be able to kick my CC addiction.

Boiling Egg Farts

When I was in a local production of the musical *The Producers*, I became incredible sick. So much so, that I ended up having to miss three performances one weekend. Missing these performances, while better in the long run, brought me into a bit of a funk.

To bring me out of this funk state, I decided to make myself some hard-boiled eggs. Yum, yum! So, around 6:00 pm on the Sunday of my last missed performance, I had just put on a couple eggs to boil when my phone rang. It was my friend Julie, who was in the show with me.

Julie: Hi Lindsay!! How are you feeling?

Me: *croaking back* I'm ok. What's up?

Julie: I'm coming over. I have to drop something off. I'll be there in 5 minutes.

Me: Oh. Ok.

Since I lived a three-minute drive from the theatre, I figured that my eggs weren't going to boil by the time she got to my place and it would be best just to leave them to boil. But, I was wrong.

Just as there's a knock on my door, my eggs start to boil.

As Julie and I were just starting to become friends, I was quite worried about what she would think of me boiling eggs. Why? Because in my drugged up and tired state I was worried that she this would be her train of thought:

OMG! This girl eats boiled eggs? That must mean she has some super nasty egg farts. Eww. I'm going to tell everyone in the cast that Lindsay has these super nasty egg farts because she eats boiled eggs.

I then feared that I would arrive at the theatre the next Wednesday, only to be ostracized by everyone because no one wanted to be around the girl who had egg farts. This thought alone should indicate how ill and drugged up I was at the time.

I decided that I would just let the eggs boil since Julie said she was just dropping something off while her hubby waited in the car.

Facing my egg judgment fear, I opened the door and there was Julie, holding out a Get Well Teddy Bear.

Me: Oh! Thank you!

Julie: You're welcome! It's from everyone in the cast hoping you get better.

Just then, the eggs start to vigorously boil. As my kitchen was right beside the front door, we both heard the eggs bouncing off one another.

Julie: What's that noise? Are you popping popcorn?

Me: Nooooo. *uncomfortably shifting from one foot to the other while blocking entrance into my home*

Julie: Then what's the noise?

Me: Umm...I'm boiling eggs. *avoiding eye contact, hanging my head in embarrassment*

Julie: Ok…

It was more than evident that I didn't really want many more questions about the eggs and that my embarrassment was at an overload. After that we quickly said our goodbyes, get wells, and see you on Wednesdays (the day of the next performance).

It took me a few more months before I finally admitted to Julie why I was so shifty about letting her know I was boiling eggs.

When I told Julie that I thought she would be disgusted in thinking that I had egg farts, she laughed so hard, tears ran down her face as snorts escaped her nose. Luckily for me, she admitted that she was a big fan of hard-boiled eggs.

She then proceeded to tell me how to make a delicious egg salad.

Since then, every time I boil an egg, I smile knowing that I have at least one friend who will completely appreciate me, even if I do end up having a nasty egg fart.

Puff Wheat Square Greatness

I hadn't seen Julie in over a month, which for us is quite rare. After texting back and forth one Tuesday morning with each other, we decided to just meet and have lunch.

Meeting at my place a half hour later, Julie sheepishly asked if we could go to Pita Pit since I always raved about how delicious it was. Naturally, I jumped at the chance to go because...YUM!

Bundling up with high neck jackets and scarves to avoid the cold Calgary January air, we wandered to the Pita Pit right by my apartment, and each chowed down on a scrumptious souvlaki pita. I was so happy to be there and see Julie's face light up as she realized the wonderful taste she was experiencing for the first time.

After our pita high, we walked down the street, soon coming upon the coffee shop where our friendship bonds grew. Since we had just eaten, I figured that we would keep walking when Julie turned to me and asked, "Can we just go in and smell it? It's been so long."

I laughed, saying yep, but secretly thought to myself, "I like this gal's style."

As soon as we walked through the door Julie promptly walked up to the counter. Quickly, I grab the last free table in the place, since we were clearly going to stay here for the rest of our chat time.

With the table secured, I wandered back up to the counter, where both Julie and I each grabbed the most delicious and large puffed wheat squares we could find. After all, we needed something to quell the garlic tzatiki sauce from our pitas that now lingered on our breath.

We sat down and started to whittle away at our blocks of puffed wheat, quickly picking up any stray puff pieces that fell during our whittling work.

After 20 minutes, we finished our squares, but not our chat.

Julie took a deep breath and snuggled her nose down into her scarf. As she came up, I noticed something had appeared on her nose. I quickly thought to myself, "What is that? Did she just magically develop a zit? NO! It's a little puffed wheat piece!"

Just as I was about to say something, Julie's eyes crossed to see what was on her nose tip. Cautiously, she pick off the puffed piece, stared at it in confusion, threw it down on the cellophane, and burst out saying, "Oh my gawd!" then went off into hysterics of laughter. She then took a breath, picked up the puff wheat piece and popped it into her mouth because they are truly that delicious.

Watching the entire time, I burst out my loud snort of a laugh and we continued this way for about 10 minutes...getting some pretty odd looks from the other tables. It was awesome laughing so hard that our abs hurt.

As we laughed, we decided that perhaps going a month without seeing one another was just too long a period. After all, who couldn't use long and loud spurts of laughter with a friend?

Who knew that one little piece of puffed wheat could make up for a lack of face time laughter over the month?

When in Doubt, Eat the Kabob!

Before starting my own company, I rarely found myself in networking situations where I had to come up with small talk. Thus, anytime I had to go to an event on behalf of the company I worked for, I wasn't my most relaxed self.

At one such particular networking I learned a valuable lesson about being myself, and making light of a situation that could have gone terribly, terribly wrong.

Back when I was working as a Marketing Specialist in corporate Calgary, I was at a networking event where lunch was served...awkwardly while standing at tiny tables where you had to mix and mingle balancing purses, notebooks, forks, knives and your graceful dignity.

This particular lunch menu focused heavily on kabobs, as most people would be inclined to pick up the stick and simply munch the meat off. I, however, would not. From the moment I got my braces in grade 7, I became someone who cuts up my food in public venues; no gnawing allowed. It was imperative I found a spot at one of the few standing tables so I could put my plate down and cut the chicken off my kabob for fear that if I bit into it, all the chicken would stick in between my teeth and I would be forced to do the awkward smile of trying to hide one's teeth the rest of the lunch. It never occurred to me that I could bite the chicken off, excuse myself from any conversation I might have been having, and gone to clean my teeth in the bathroom.

I thought luck was with me that day as I found a spot beside a lovely lady from another company. As I was working my chicken off my kabob, we exchanged pleasantries, talking about the event we were at, where each other worked, and so forth. All of a sudden, as I worked a particularly difficult piece of chicken from the kabob stick, I saw it fly off my stick and land on this lady's plate. We both stopped for a moment, staring at the chicken, not sure how to react.

Finally, I haltingly laughed out, "Sorry, but the chicken is so good. I thought you might like to try it!" She had a little chortle and we continued on our conversation (although I had stopped eating the chicken from that point on). At the end of the conversation she looked at me and pointedly asked, "Would you be interested in leaving your current job? We're looking to hire a good Marketing Specialist and I think you'd be a good fit with our team." While I was flattered, I said I wasn't looking at the moment.

While the flying chicken could have been a disaster, it ended up being laughed off and turned into a potential job offer!

The biggest lesson was that just because I messed up, I apologized, showed my personality and moved on. That was all I could do, other than offer the woman chicken.

After all, as I would certainly come to realize as I grew my own business, networking is about building relationships and the only way you can do that is if you show WHO you are and how you react in awkward situations.

Ever since this Chicken Moment happened, I've gone to networking lunches keeping the following in mind:

1. Breath; everyone there is in the same boat when it comes to small chit chat,
2. Laugh at yourself; it's endearing, people can relate to you better, and it makes situations a wee less awkward, and
3. Learn to take a bit bite; if you're going to have a kabob, for goodness sake, chew the meat off, and then go floss!

Food Lessons: Food for Thought

- Food is about so much more than sustenance. It's about memories. What memories and emotions are tied to your food – good and bad?
- NEVER comment on the speed at which women eat their cake.
- Everybody's nose is different (much like the Poop Lesson of no one but you is aware of certain smells).
- Candy is physically dangerous in more ways than one...but boy oh boy, candy corn sure is good.
- Embarrassing food situations make for great connection / bonding opportunities. You just have to start paying attention.

Number 3: Time for Your Relief

And with that, my constipation relief stories come to an end – for now. These stories truly helped bring me out of my despair. They helped me to focus on the awkward, the ridiculous, the absurd, the laughter, and everything in between. A time when all I wanted was to not exist and couldn't fully feel, these stories reminded me of what it meant to exist and all feelings are meant to be felt.

Purposely looking for the humour in the mundane helped me move through my constipated brain to a much healthier flow of thought.

I'm not saying that I've had a steadily healthy movement of brain waves since, after all, constipation ebbs and flows; however, I've been able to recognize what my brain's "prunes" are to start the movement.

So, how do you create your own constipated brain relief?

If you're feeling brain clogged, and struggling to get some healthy movement through your own cotton-filled brain, first off know that it's okay. You are not alone in this, but only you can truly figure out what works for you in getting the brain flow to happen.

Start with trying to focus on what your own individual brain fibre is. While this will be different for everyone – for me it was writing, for a friend of mine it was exercise, for another, it was Emotional Freedom Technique (more commonly referred to as EFT) – it is clear that no one way is the right way for everyone. Below are a few ideas on how, when you're ready, you can start your own mineral oil for the mind.

- **Talk to someone**. As simple as this sounds, talking is what got me to start sorting through the muck in my head. You'd be surprised at who will not just listen, but understand and encourage.

- **Speak to a professional**. Of course, speaking with friends and family helps you feel supported, however, having a truly objective individual listen and seeing your uniqueness for the first time can sometimes be the different perspective you need. It wasn't until my psychologist pointed out my odd sense of humour that I started to write down the stories that would help me move forward.

- **Journal**. I know, I know – everyone says journal. But, from my own experience, this has helped all the negative fog have a place to go. I have pages plastered with negativity. While this may seem like the opposite of what you want, you are actually giving your negativity a place to escape from inside your brain. No longer will the negative thoughts be clambering around, ringing constantly in your ears. Clearing out the negative allows you to start anew in your head. You will most likely have to do this multiple times (I still do negative spews), but you give yourself permission to let it out, without judgement.

  When you feel ready and / or strong enough, you can go back and read them to see where the truth lies in these thoughts. I suggest reading them out loud, as the power of these thoughts begins to dwindle simply because you most likely would never say these thoughts to a friend. Treat yourself like you would your friend. Not only that, but by reading these entries when you are in a clearer headspace, you'll be able to see that the words of negativity you wrote aren't true. That these negative thoughts no longer have a purpose for you and you can start to rewrite the scripts of who you truly are - most likely a strong and unique individual who has the power to conquer demons.

- **Discover your constipation relief**. For me, it was writing humour about the mundane. For you, it could be something as simple as doing your nails, building play doh statues, or just tying a spectacular shoelace. Whatever gives you a burst of, "yep. That moment was an okay moment," look to understand why. Moving through your own depression constipation won't be an explosive event, but little movements along the way. Whatever gives you the slightest bit of positive relief is worth looking into.

The biggest thing to know is that you are not alone (so very cliché...but so very true).

While it will be a road from feeling completely stuck to consistent flow, I have total faith that you will finally have your own amazing brain poop and be able to start moving forward again with a sense of relief.

Thank Yous

Of course, there comes a time when you just have to say thank you to those who stood by you and simply held your hand…while silently encouraging you.

To Andy: Thank you for reminding me what it means to laugh and not questioning the tears, but providing the tissues.

To Mom & Dad: Thank you for being the amazing people you are and for supporting me in my darkest hours. Somehow I hit the jackpot with you as my parents.

To Robin: My own bird of music. Thank you for being my little big sister and understanding our odd, quirky, Harle brains.

To Coco and Chase: the puppies who taught me what truly unconditional love means…and that no matter who you are, you are worthy of love.

To countless friends for their support, stories, and hugs: Megan, Diana, Naomi, Andrea, Amanda, Lisa, Nicole, Brigitte, Susan, and Lisel.

To you, yep you! Reading right now! Thank you for taking the time for yourself. I hope you've had a few giggles while reading this, and are ready to find your own prune juice to get your flow going again.

Love always,
Lindsay

About the Author

Lindsay Harle-Kadatz is the owner of The Write Harle, helping businesses refine their voice and brand message through content. When not doing this, she spends time with her hubby, Andy, and their two fur babies, Chase and Coco. With everything, Lindsay continues to make puns and look for the funny in the mundane.

Always looking to connect, share ideas, and hear your stories, you can contact Lindsay by:

Email: lindsay@thewriteharle.com
Twitter: @thewriteharle
Website: www.thewriteharle.com

CPSIA information can be obtained
at www.ICGtesting.com
Printed in the USA
LVOW11s1416011116
511193LV00001B/113/P

9 781537 535043